ROOKIE: SELECTED POEMS

Caroline Bird is a poet and playwright. Her 2020 collection, *The Air Year*, won the Forward Prize for Best Collection 2020 and was shortlisted for the Polari Prize and the Costa Prize. Her fifth collection, *In These Days of Prohibition*, was shortlisted for the 2017 T.S. Eliot Prize and the Ted Hughes Award. A two-time winner of the Foyle Young Poets Award, her first collection, *Looking Through Letterboxes*, was published in 2002 when she was fifteen. She won an Eric Gregory Award in 2002 and was shortlisted for the Geoffrey Dearmer Prize in 2001 and the Dylan Thomas Prize in 2008 and 2010. As a playwright, Bird has been shortlisted for the George Devine Award and the Susan Smith Blackburn Prize. Her theatre credits include: *The Trojan Women* (Gate Theatre, 2012), *The Trial of Dennis the Menace* (Purcell Room, 2012), *Chamber Piece* (Lyric Hammersmith, 2013), *The Wonderful Wizard of Oz* (Northern Stage, 2015), *The Iphigenia Quartet* (Gate Theatre, 2016) and *Red Ellen* (Northern Stage, Nottingham Playhouse, Royal Lyceum Theatre and York Theatre Royal, 2022). She was one of the five official poets at the 2012 London Olympics.

ROOKIE

Selected Poems

Caroline Bird

CARCANET POETRY

'Now when I address you
it is somebody else speaking.
I couldn't be in two places at once, could I?
You sound like a real fruitcake, man.'

— James Tate

First published in Great Britain in 2022 by
Carcanet
Alliance House, 30 Cross Street
Manchester, M2 7AQ
www.carcanet.co.uk

A CIP catalogue record for this book is
available from the British Library.

ISBN 978 1 80017 186 2

Book design by Andrew Latimer
Printed in Great Britain by SRP Ltd, Exeter, Devon

The publisher acknowledges financial
assistance from Arts Council England.

Contents

From 'IN THESE DAYS OF PROHIBITION' (2017)

From 'THE AIR YEAR' (2020)

ROOKIE: SELECTED POEMS

FROM 'LOOKING THROUGH LETTERBOXES' (2002)

GEOGRAPHY LESSONS

When you've reached the peak,
the summit, the end,
you've come to the limit,
let me tell you gently
that the world is round, my sweet,
and it's all a long walk backwards,
starting from here.

I KNOW THIS BECAUSE YOU TOLD ME

I'll break my neck if I jump again from the top of these stairs.
I'll suffer for the rest of my life in hospital
if I put my finger up my nose and then the wind changes.
I know this because you told me.

I'll drown if I jump once more in this nice muddy puddle,
there'll be a flash flood and the rain will rise and take us all.
The world should live in perfect harmony
and you'll kill the bloody neighbours if they don't trim their hedge.

I should never swear, I know this because you told me.
If I talk to the teachers about our mortgage and the fact
that we don't pay our bills, then a monster will come out of the toilet
in the dead of night and pull me down.

You are not joking and only want to warn me. You are a good parent
and tell me life as it is, I know this because you told me.
If I fall in love at seventeen then it will not last.
If I eat too much I will explode and muck up your new shirt.

If I burp then I will blow myself inside out. The world
is quite a strange place and everyone is strange except you.
I know this because you told me.
If I take money from your wallet, it is called crime,

if you take money from my piggy bank, it is called borrowing.
If I never have a bath I will smell and people won't walk
on the same side of the street as me,
but if I do then I'll be sucked down the plughole. Some women shave.

I know this because you told me. The banister is for holding,
not for sliding down and you were never rude to your parents.
I will break my neck if I jump again from the top of these stairs
and no, I should not do it anyway.

DUSK AND PETROL

If you cross your eyes slightly then the lawn is on fire.
I stir my coffee twice and wait for it to settle
as the man on the radio with a voice like sinking bread
tells the nation that dousing yourself in petrol
isn't a good thing to do. Spontaneous rainfalls of rolling eyes
are swooping across the country, they see everything,
so don't go out of the house, don't stay in the house,
don't move, run for your life. My coffee is too hot,
I now have a mouth like the bottom of a steaming pipe
and it's too early to go to bed. I think about hospitals
to pass the time, think about memories seeping
through scars, think about fainting surgeons.
The doctors said there was nothing they could do.
Why do we have doctors that can't do anything?
Can they walk, talk, keep a clean house?
The lawn is burning itself out now. I pick up the phone
then put it down. I find it much easier to make enemies,
I can make them out of gingerbread, playdoh, leaves,
I can model them to look like you.
I can place them face-down in the sink.

GINGERBREAD HOUSE

He smelt of 'fresh from the oven' adulthood,
his tongue on the hinge of his lips, his eyes spinning
with sex and cinnamon as he invited you in.
You gazed with wonder at his gingerbread house,
rocking back on your heels with childish delight.
You took a long drag on your lollypop stick
then flicked it away.
Later you spat it all back out to your friends,
showed them the goodies you'd brought back
hidden underneath your tongue. You licked
their pink bedrooms with your knowledge,
spread your laughter thumb-deep on their walls,
tasted the irony on your teeth.

Look little children, come peek at the trail of bread,
look how the teeth marks are still fresh
since they were ripped from the loaf,
look how the birds swoop, hundreds and thousands
of hungry red mouths.

Liquorice doormat, sherbet-coated window pane,
marzipan-stained glass, milk chocolate letterbox,
gingerbread door. His hair like spun sugar
in your hands.
More cream in your coffee dear?
You really are the sweetest child.

Running through the forest, the soft breeze
at each girl's back, like the sound of fairies' wings.
Swooping, diving, disappearing in the shadows,
they come like wolves to the house where he sleeps.

The wizard, the prince, the eldest son
and as his walls are eaten from around his bed,
he dreams of adult things, running, swooping,
diving and of how the sugar doesn't taste as sweet
once you've gorged, indulged, stuffed yourself
with every crumb, every lick and strip.
Left not a single melting piece untouched.
He smelt of 'fresh from the oven' adulthood.
They eat him too, his pale skin vibrates in their fingers
and the rain falls on his mattress and the place
where his house used to be.

At last, licking their lips, they return to the forest,
no longer wolves, just girls. They look for their path
through the night. Lost. They blame the robins,
they blame the swallows, they blame the swans,
the eagles, they blame the vultures
and their hungry red mouths.

Thirty paperclip statues on every table in the house
and things are slightly boring without you.
I've knitted a multi-coloured jacket for every woodlouse
in the park. But what can you do?

I've given all the cracks in the pavement pet names
and taken snapshots of individual specks of dust,
I'm not a trainspotter and deny all those claims
but have developed an interest in rust.

The budgies in the pet shop now speak fluent French
and I have made friends with a golf commentator.
I was restless one evening so dug a fifty-foot trench
then filled it in ten seconds later.

I drank ninety cups of tea in one afternoon
and filled the kettle by collecting drops of dew.
Gardeners' Question Time is on really soon
and things are slightly boring without you.

MULTITUDE

An army of you, hiding at the back of my eyes
on the curve of my iris, trampolining.
I'm loping again down a street
much like the one on the letter.
The one dusting itself at the foot of my bed,
steaming with commas and question marks.
Your road is claustrophobic,
when I reach your house it'll just be a straw
sucked on by sky. I have hands like slaughter,
I have blood on my chest, the left-hand side,
it's gleaming like boiling red butter.
I have internal bruises too, just inside my ribs,
just below my shoulder.
I wish your house would puff away in a cloud
of transparent smoke, would leave me standing here
like a pole staring into space.
But it's getting larger with every lope I take.
The dandelions in the garden have your face,
they frown and shake their heads.
Even the dog dirt looks like you.
How come you have such a big door?
Brass handles, padlocks and chains,
an inch of barbed wire over each daffodil,
each flower and weed. I knock, hoping
for some reason, that I might answer the door myself,
and that I might be you, coming to talk it over.

OWL POEM

I refuse to write a poem about an owl,
better to write about a person with an owl
or a person who wants an owl, or better still,
a person who hates owls and will never
have an owl.

PLAYING AT FAMILIES

When you can pick up your mother in thickset hands,
roll her over and tenderly remove her wings.

When you can rip off your father's moustache
with a twitch of finger and thumb,

telling him, 'It'll never do good with the ladies,
not anymore.'

When you can place them on your shelf
like miniature models, knowing that every night

they search the bedroom,
looking for lovers and empty wine bottles

but melt into the carpet when you open your eyes.
When you can arrange your grandparents in tiny velvet chairs

and gently put them in the embers of the fire,
soothing them through cooing lips

that you're 'Well fed and educated,' so there's no need to worry.
When you can put your relatives in separate boxes

to make sure they don't breed or cut each other's hair
while you're out of the house.

When you can lift them, light as a feather, kiss them
and tuck them in matchbox beds,

making sure your family are locked in innocent slumber,
before leaving to go clubbing every night.

When you can do all this, then you have to face the guilt
when finally, after too many years, you creep back in

to find each wide awake and crying
that they hadn't known where you were.

I CAME TO SEE IF YOU WERE OK

I came to see if you were OK
not because I'm bothered but because
my mate asked me to because he
had something to do that probably
could have waited until tomorrow
and all that but he wasn't going to
come anyway but his mum said
or something but anyway I was
asked to tell you, at least I think
I've remembered it right, that there's
no need to be down and stuff
because we'll always be your friends.
Um... I'm not actually part of that
we because I don't know you.
Anyway you look OK.

YOUR HEARTBREAK

No one else is having your heartbreak.
Your perfect pulsing peach
in scarlet syrup,
your creamy self
pitying.

Not even when the whole world
is stacked like chairs
and you are milky-eyed
with sleep, honey, chocolate,
blues before bedtime.

Right here, where your hand is,
all yours. A beautiful, bleeding,
sprouting red roses,
picked in two halves
from the heartbreak tree,
heartbreak.

It is your prize, you've earned it,
heaved it up
from the wishing well
of your throat,
held its broken body,
treasured it, fed it with tears
the size of cupcakes
and nights like shining spoons.

No one else is having your heartbreak.
Or the way it makes the sound of horses's hooves
if you hold a piece in either hand
and bang it together like a coconut.

Even the rain was throwing back its head.
I never knew I was so funny. They were pulling out their hair
in clumps and stuffing it in their mouths, they were sitting
on windowsills and falling out of windows.
I can't quite remember how it started,
maybe when the bedclothes tittered as I headed for the sink
and the toothbrush chattered on my teeth.

When I reached the foot of the stairs,
the girl with the ponytail choked on her own tongue
and the man with the face like a paving slab cracked up.
Suddenly I was hilarious. I was perched cross-
legged on the sofa,
the sky collapsing down into the drains,
I had everyone from the neighbourhood gathered
around my ankles, bursting.
I had them all in stitches just by twitching my eye.

But the rain stopped at midnight.
By this time their throats were bleeding
and helicopters had sifted people in from around the globe,
just to catch a glimpse.
But when the rain died there was silence.
Then shaking of heads,
and the stepping back into of planes.
After, it was kind of a shock
when I placed a mug on the table and nobody laughed.

BUBBLE BATH

Like shattered glass, we went our different ways,
you across the bridge and down where the traffic was,
me, down an alleyway without an address.
Now, you could pass me in the street. The letter
was frank and without emotion, written on the back
of a napkin while you washed the dishes, typed
with one finger fumbling the keys. That's rich that is,
stroke my hair like I was bubble bath, then brisk home
through the trees, where the fountains run frozen
and the breeze changes the shape of your face.

FROM 'TROUBLE CAME TO THE TURNIP' (2006)

MY LOVE MADE ME A HAT

First you had to catch the bee,
running around in meadows with a net,
skimming down hills on your grazed little knees.
You picked an angry one,
one with bad childhood memories,
pent-up aggression,
ideas beyond its station.
A bee with plenty to prove.

The next bit was easier,
some shops still sell them,
something from a costume drama,
something stiff and lacy
with hard, pearl-bone fasteners.
Something with a hatred for heads.
A bonnet with a complex.

Then you had to pin me down.
I thought you were randy,
I didn't know you were furious.
When you pulled out the gaffer tape,
I said 'Oh baby.'

Now I can't stop slapping my face.
My eyes are swollen to the size of bicycle wheels.
I flap about the yard,
this honey bleeding from my ears,
this terrible, terrible buzzing.
And every day is a summer's day.

THE MISTRESS OF THE HOUSE

The mistress of the house is scared of houses.
She has filled the bedroom with giant electric fans.
She has carpeted the ceiling with cottonwool clouds.
She's been sneaking grass cuttings from the garden
and grazing in the lounge.
She's been sledging down the stairs on a tea-tray,
yelling up the chimney. The tables are boats.
The oven stinks of frying beach balls.
Jackets are strewn across the hallway like puddles,
the taps are always running.
She scrapes her fingernails down bars
of cooking chocolate, bangs saucepans together
then hides under the bed screaming, 'Black out! Black out!'

The mistress of the house is scared of people.
Her podgy husband brings her rainwater
in plastic bags. Sometimes he smells of trains
or pubs, or men, or schoolgirls.
She can distinguish the smells. They dry her blood.
He has a job in the city. She knows about the city.
The city is run by dinosaurs in spiky hats
who breathe sewage into suitcases.
She knows the danger that lurks beyond the garden gnomes.
She can hear the rumble of lava
from the core of the earth.

The mistress of the house is scared of birdsong
Her podgy husband used to screw her with the great outdoors.
His mouth used to bubble with buttercups and summer hazes.
Now, the cameras in the wallpaper are sleeping and sick.
He works all day while she plays in the bath

with an oar and a sailor's cap.
Once she tried dressing up in a suit
and seducing the servant girl.
But they don't have a servant girl.
So she spun around the conservatory, making siren noises,
handcuffing herself to chairs.

The mistress of the house reads her husband's diary.
She dips his toothbrushes in the toilet.
What kind of husband keeps a diary?
He doesn't even use her name.
He refers to her as 'M.H.'
He writes, 'Someday I'm going to wake up
and find myself a real woman.'
She's a shadow on the mattress, an arm in the dark.

The mistress of the house wonders about killing herself
or eating herself, or burning a piece of her foot.
She is Elizabeth the First. She is Sinbad. She is a nympho nun
swinging from the vines of a medieval vineyard
with a sword in her mouth. She is Donald fucking Duck.
She wants to be born again, as a polar bear,
and live beneath an avalanche
in a state of joyous collapse
with a furry face to soak her tears.

The mistress of the house is scared of moonshine,
roast dinners and post.
There will be no divine intervention.
The plugs are sick of electricity.
See how the coffee table creeps around the room?
See how the mistress of the house
carries it on her back like a coffin?
She has armed herself with sticks.
She is ready for bed.

SHINY BIN

When you graduated
your parents bought you a shiny bin
with a pedal.
I remembered you on the plane,
playing the invisible piano
on the flap-down table. When I die
I want to be an amusing anecdote.
Your parents had plans for that bin,
the shiny bin with the sensible
pop-up lid. Oh, it was so shiny.
Oh, it was everything you'd ask for
in a bin. It was a lovely bin.
Some of the other daughters
got inflatable chairs, those
who thought 'knuckling down' involved
sitting in circles and introducing themselves.
The ones with the beanbags.
I remembered you on the plane,
suddenly longing for a straggly beard
to dip into your coffee
and be wise behind. To have kind eyes.
But you were a girl,
a girl with a shiny bin.

Leopold adores the Deserter's wife.
They swear eternal love, although his regiment leaves tonight.

The two assassins lead Eudoxie to the madhouse,
her face scooped with hunger and haunting grey light.

Rachel is sentenced to death by Cardinal Brodel
for consorting with a Christian. The General regains his sight.

The Englishman is wounded during a procession.
Lakme eats a leaf from the poisonous datura tree.

I know you think you like me.

Senta and the Dutchman will always be apart.
She can only find salvation through her love. The General is not a spy

though they metaphorically drown him in the ocean,
bury his body in floating white sheets. The years go by.

A blood-encrusted soprano is carried to the cauldron.
Eleazer fetches water from the holy spring.

I know you are sometimes passionate.
(The minstrel flees the monastery to rescue his king.)

I know you often slam the door.
I know your bed is hard.

Vreli and Sali unite in death,
burn slowly down the river in a barge.

I know you wake up frowning. I know stuff is unfair.
Aschenbach slumps dead in his deckchair.

A SEASONAL SURPRISE FOR MISS PRINGLE

It was Christmas and the Wibbles were singing carols
to their pig. Miss Pringle was slicing pumpernickel,
thinking fondly of her seven lovely daughters,
each so rum-faced and rosy, cheerful and chirpy,

who were waiting inside the cardboard cake,
ready to spring out with whoops and festive frolics
upon some unsuspecting reveller
but they'd been there since November

and were losing oxygen. Miss Pringle anointed
the tiger prawns with truffle oil, topped off the turkey
with an olive swirl, and was none the wiser
while, from beneath the tree, came the sound

of a tiny mouse, a very tiny mouse, convulsing,
spasmodically, in his tiny mousetrap.
Then, all at once, the doorbell tinkled and a hoard
of lively do-gooders burst into the room, babbling

warmly and bearing gifts of scones and vegetable
filo tartlets. What a vivacious bunch! There was
Catherine Crumb, the baker, Bertie Barrel, the bartender,
Sherman Sherbet, the confectioner, and Gertrude Gimble,

an assistant executive hygiene operative for a law firm in Kent.
Each held a candle and each held a hymn book,
their cheeks aflame with sheer delight
for they had come with a special treat for Miss Pringle!

Yesterday (they sang) a boat docked in the harbour –
a beautiful boat with velvet sails, wavy-haired cabin boys
and mermaids carved into the mast...
Miss Pringle stopped them mid-flow.

'Oh, can it be?' she cried, eyelids all a flutter,
'That my darling son, John, has arrived safely home?
After not a word of news in ten years?
Endlessly pacing the house, wringing my hands and praying

for the kindness of the ocean, he has returned,
laden with gold, exotic fruits and cinnamon tobacco?
My life and soul, my child, home in time for Christmas?
Can it really be true?'

Mr Barrel smiled, and said no.
The boat had been transporting donkeys from Calais.
However, they had bought her a donkey.
They thought it would help with heavy shopping

and long-distance journeys. It was roped outside
and answered to the name of Valerie.
Miss Pringle thanked them kindly and poured the eggnog.
They settled down to wait for snow.

MARY-JANE

She was born as identical twins.
Two bodies in one body.
Two brains in one skull.
Mary liked to stand on the roof and wave her pants at helicopters.
Jane liked to lie on her back in the cellar, pretending to be a bug.
Mary liked to cycle naked to school.
Jane wore clothes in the bath.
Mary dreamt of big men with big bulges.
Jane dreamt she had a bucket for a head.
They tried to compromise.
Mary tried to settle it with an arm-wrestle.
Jane tried to settle it by crying and crying and crying.
Jane woke up with a pillow shoved down hard on her face
and the sound of Mary coughing.
Jane crept out one night and ran until her feet grew engines.
Mary woke with blisters.
They sometimes make love,
they sometimes try to cut themselves apart
but Mary-Jane is no doctor.

LOVE HAS ARRIVED

The petrol leaks from runaway cars
and children jive in puddles
donning emerald petrol slippers,
saying hello in different languages,
saying just enough.
The buildings pour out from their windows
spreading oozing concrete joy
across the shivering midnight grass
and you have come
to put things right, to thread the beads,
come far across the desert
with spit on your handkerchief
to wipe my eyes, to wipe your own,
you have arrived.
The city moans and rolls and tucks her knees,
a cardboard box stretches out into a hotel,
all the clocks throw up their hands
and yawn lethargic timeless chimes.
I won't be satisfied.
I can't bend over a chair and fill with sighs,
I can't seed the sweaty fruit of strawberry palms,
this is not a love that can be peeled
and scoffed in segments,
this is not a love between two people,
this is a ferris wheel with a suitcase, boarding a train,
this is a bolt of lightning waiting in a bowl,
this is my soul colliding with a lamppost,
this is... oh.

I'm leaning on this balcony,
like my ancestors used to do
with hair and thoughts like mine
in the days when you could slot
your pain inside a straw
and blow your pea-size woe
across the spongy evening traffic
and the relief was electric
and you could turn your life on a pin
and you could get water from a tap
without signing anything
and you could leave your blood where it is,
a vase could be a hat,
you could have a decent kid
and light was solid,
you could buy it from corner shops
in paper bags of blinding shards
and I could take your glorious head,
hold it high above my glorious head
and you would see everything
the way I see it
and you would be appalled.

Love has arrived in the city,
it's a glorious day, love has arrived,
they announce it over the tannoy,
love has arrived at platform six,
make way for love, love coming through,
step aside please Sir, clear the aisles,
if you'd be so kind as to remove that bag,
love is in the building, show some respect,

stand back Madam, I don't appreciate
people breathing on me, love is on its way,
that's right, stay behind the line, don't want to frighten
the poor bugger, put that thing away,
what in the name of... get your fucking arm
out of my face... love has arrived.

THE PLAGUE

It takes more than pants and zips
to hide my cunt, it yells in its sleep,
the town is bucking, villagers
are pillaging each other. The bodies
pile up, threesomes become foursomes,
the priest fucked a firework, a second
coming, a third, it's a plague, seven
dwarves in one bed, the policemen
have permanent erections, no one
has any blood in their heads,
the vet does curious things to a horse,
a mattress outside every bank,
there's no point trying to read a book
not unless you take it from behind.
Someone fetch a bucket, a bible, a plug,
a hook to hang these fidgeting frocks,
even that scabby tortoise looks sexy,
my leg has burnt a hole in my trousers.

VIRGIN

If I was a virgin, I could streak across your garden,
drape myself across your armchair like a portrait of a lady
who is unabashed and simple as a cherry in a bowl
and only dreams of ponies and weekends by the seaside,
sipping unchartered water from a baby-blue decanter,
sighing with her slender throat and saving herself.

If I was a virgin, I could wear white in winter,
read your dirty magazines with a shy and puzzled look,
like I didn't know a crotch from a coffee table, darling
I could scream blue bloody murder
when you caught me in the shower,
snatch a towel around my outraged breast,
my eyes awash with droplet tears.
I wouldn't hold your hand in public, if I was a virgin,
I would never spill spaghetti on my jeans.
My voice would be as gentle as an angel blowing bubbles.
I would be terrified by frisbees and sports of any kind.
I would always ride my bicycle side-saddle.

If I was a virgin, I'd look great in a bikini.
I'd feed you grapes and rye bread
and my hands would smell of soap.
You would hold me in your arms like a precious piece of crockery,
I would sob into your jacket, you would gasp inside your pants.

If I was a virgin, you wouldn't look at other girls,
you would spring clean your apartment
before you asked me round for supper,
give me your bed, spend the night on the sofa,
dreaming of the gentle way I breathed inside my bra,

my nightgown would remind you of fragrant summer orchards
and nobody would know my mouth tastes of peaches
and I thrash in my sleep like a baboon.

Sorry for waking you up twelve times in one night
to polish my flip-flops.
Sorry for comparing your collarbone to a coat hanger.
Sorry for building council flats on the bones of our bed.
Sorry for sewing up every orifice
then getting all naked.
Sorry for appearing at your door like the Resurrection
expecting clean underwear and videos.
Sorry for using your gravestone as a clothes horse.
Sorry for sticking a telescope inside you without asking.
Sorry for eating lard in the toilets of your gym.
Sorry for balancing an apple on your head
then shooting you in the cheek.
Sorry for writing the Magna Carta in a made-up language.
Sorry for cutting myself into six bloody chunks
then slamming them all on different trains.
Sorry for unzipping you at school proms
then refusing to be unzipped.
Sorry for lining your helter-skelter with sandpaper.
Sorry for strutting down your road with a plague-ridden cart
piling up the bodies before they were dead.
Sorry for mistaking your eyes for obscene blemishes.
Sorry for leaving you quivering by the fire escape
while I bonked in a taxi.
Sorry for urging your therapist to ignore you.
Sorry for telling you I needed space
then playing twister with football teams in bobsleighs.
Sorry for mistaking your veins for poisonous eels.
Sorry for attaching your chihuahua to an electric whisk.
Sorry for plugging in my headphones at your murder trial.
Sorry for listening intently to your problems

then fobbing you off with a punchbag and a drum.
Sorry for making you do backflips in a small metal box.
Sorry for locking you in a cell with a blindfolded tattooist.
Sorry for eating shit and borrowing your toothbrush.
Sorry for squatting you beneath tables at dinner parties.
Sorry for feeding the leftovers to the dog.
Sorry for fingering your neighbours
then brushing back your hair.
Sorry for loving you with every freckle on my tongue.
Sorry for my bloodless little smile.
Sorry for the wet on my face.
Sorry for making the right choice at the right time
in completely good faith.

MOPE

Sometimes the day goes silent, mouths
move in the street, people change, glide,
the click of a new slide in the projector,
chewing gum loses its flavour, people
kiss now, talk later, watch through glass,
pass through, pasteurise, curtains twitch
behind averted eyes, everyone is looking
for a word that isn't love, because love
is loud and the roads are blanketed,
we pick up the phone just to listen,
it takes research, graphs, ammunition
to say goodbye, each sentence requires
a hundred more, but darling,
my tongue is sore, I want to lie you down,
here on the pavement, put my head
on your neck like there's a geyser beneath us
that could flood the whole town,
sometimes the day stops, people freeze,
one foot on the bus, or standing in crowds
holding bottles in the air like realising
your skirt has been unravelling since
breakfast, and the day empties out, lifts
upside down, shakes like a purse, my lip
is burnt, my clothes smell of smoke again
and I love you, it's raining, just look at the rain.

RELATIONSHIP DOLLS

I was thinking about opening a doll factory.
Grumpy, tired-looking dolls
with messy hair and scowling teeth.
Talking dolls. Dolls that talk
and talk and talk. You pull a string
from their spine and they scream
'This just isn't working'
'Where am I going with my life?'
or 'I need some time alone.'
Dolls that cry until you stamp on them.
Dolls that need thirty-seven batteries
just to keep going. Dolls that come
with baggage, piles and piles of useless
accessories, guaranteed to clutter
every inch of your house. Each doll
will be unique, some with bust noses,
some with scarred wrists, all with broken
hearts that tumble from their chests
when you burp them. Don't burp them.
Dolls that won't be patronised. Dolls
with revolving heads, dolls that will sit
on your pillow and watch you while you sleep.
Why would you buy such a doll?
Why spend your money, *all* your money,
on a doll like this? A doll that will drink
your gin, forbid you to touch other dolls,
a doll that will insist upon marriage,
a doll you can rest in the crook of your arm,
a lover you can legally drown.

THE LADY WITH THE LAMP

Someone threw a brick at her window
and she caught it, mid-air, in one hand.
She made a perfect tuna sandwich.
A fly buzzed around her plate
and she tapped it on the head with a spoon.

In the morning she bought a pair of shoes,
walked to the beach
then tossed her shoes in the sea.
She felt the sand between her toes
as she unbuttoned her shirt.
A man said, 'Nice tits',
and she said, 'Thank you.'
She ate half a croissant
and gave the other half to a seagull.

That night, she started her period
and left a small saucer of blood on the balcony
for the mosquitoes.
She enjoyed the first page of a book,
ripped it out and pinned it on the bathroom door
so she could read it again later.
A childhood friend dropped by to apologise
and she accepted their apology.
She draped her pants over the radiator.

In the morning she had warm pants.
She took the bus to the city
and gave up her seat for a teenager
with a heavy skateboard.
A stranger showed her his holiday photos

and she was genuinely interested.
She went window-shopping
and allowed herself to be attracted to a mannequin.
She banged her elbow on a lamppost
and didn't blame the lamppost.
She sat by a fountain and smiled at the tourists.
She watched someone's bags
while they went to the loo.

That night, she made a lantern
out of yellow sugar paper
and placed it over a candle.
She poured a modest portion of pasta
into a saucepan.
The saucepan still contained traces
of yesterday's chicken soup
but this added flavour to the pasta.
She had a bath and shaved delicately around her ankles.
She enjoyed having smooth ankles.
She rolled a thin cigarette whilst choosing her pyjamas.
She chose purple silk.
She checked her watch and unlocked the door.

At midnight exactly, her lover walked in.
They proceeded to embrace.
They kissed with tongues
and didn't clash teeth, not even once.
They moved into the bedroom
and ruffled the sheets.
They moaned, but not too loud
because her neighbours were asleep.
They rubbed noses and ate a few strawberries.
She opened the window
so they could smell the honeysuckle.

She stood naked in the moonlight like a swan.
She said, 'Isn't it funny how the world falls into place?'
Her lover said, 'I love you',
and she frowned.

In the morning, her lover made her breakfast
and she ate more than she wanted,
to be polite.
Her lover suggested a trip to the zoo
and she left the house without washing her hair.
They strolled around the zoo, holding hands.
She wanted to free the monkeys
but the cages were locked.
Later, they shared a cocktail in a bar
and the waiter gave them two straws.
Her lover drank quicker than she did
and she barely got a taste.
She had to help her lover into the taxi.
The leather seats were sticky on her thighs.
On the journey, her lover told her a story
about a girl who had sex with cucumbers.
Her lover found this very funny.

That night, she put her vegetables in the bin.
Her lover sat with her on the sofa
and dented a few of her cushions.
During the television commercials
she began to tweeze her eyebrows in the mirror
but her lover said her eyebrows looked perfect
and then lit a cigarette in her living room
without asking.

In the morning, she went for a jog.
Her lover was fast asleep
with one arm on her side of the bed.
She jogged to the supermarket
and bought a fresh baguette
and some moisturiser for her legs.
She spoke in French to the French shop assistant.
She held the door for a man with a walking stick.
She jogged to the river and fed the bread to the ducks.
She broke a twig from a tree
and drew a heart in the mud.
She looked at the heart and felt the sun on her neck.
She forgot all about her lover.

That night, her lover had a nosebleed
and the blood fell on the bathroom tiles.
She wiped off the blood with a dishcloth
and her dishcloth was ruined.
Her lover couldn't be more sorry.
Her lover bought her a bouquet of crimson flowers
that stood on the kitchen table like a sore thumb.
She tried to do some breathing exercises to calm herself down
but her lover joined in.

In the morning, her lover wanted sex.
She got up to freshen her breath
but her lover said, 'I don't mind.'
She sat on the edge of the bed and began to cry.
Her lover held her tight and rocked her like a baby.
Her lover didn't ask her to explain.
This made her cry even more.

That night, she didn't bother
to leave out any bird-seed for the birds.
She opened the door
and told her lover to get out.
Her lover said, 'I love you,'
and she said, 'Goodbye.'
She watched her lover crumble down the drive.
She waited until her house was quiet.
She chose her red velvet pyjamas.
She read the second page of her book.
She slipped between the sheets like a wave
and dreamt that she was Florence Nightingale
and all the soldiers were thanking her.

THE LEPRECHAUN THINKS IT MATTERS

The leprechaun thinks it matters
because it matters to her.
She wraps her legs around the gold.
She thinks someone will find her.
And she's so pretty, sitting there
with her battered little pot,
and her battered little smile,
with the rainbow exploding from her chest.
She doesn't know that it's impossible,
the storybooks told her
there would be a prince, or a princess
or a weary peasant with a stick.
The rest of the leprechaun tribe
called her The Chosen One,
they said people would spend their lives searching,
they said that she alone knew the answer
and then they left her
with her battered little pot
and her battered little smile,
wondering what they expected her to do.

BREAD

I wish to only need bread.
To love in return for a loaf.
To have a hat. To doff my hat.
I wish to have a friend called Larry.
I wish me and Larry could sit
quietly and eat our bread.
Slowly, with our fingers,
or with big chunky forks.
Arrange my bread
on the floor and sing to it.
Sing to my bread.
Eat my bread in little chews.
No conversation. No contact.
Just bread and looking out of windows.
Thinking of bread. I wish
to cherish you, or Larry, or anyone
with a blind bread love
that is fresh and plain
and steady on the stomach.
A love that never hurts or changes.
A love based on bread. Giving
bread, receiving bread,
bread fluffing down from the sky.
I wish to only need bread.
I wish to be bread.

THE FAIRY IS BORED WITH HER GARDEN

The fairy is bored with her garden,
bored with flying around, bored with twinkling,
bored with having sex with drunk people
just because they make good promises.
They work so hard to get her.
They smoke and swallow and knock them back.
They say, 'This time, I'm not leaving.'
They stroke her trembling ears.
Every night she elopes,
expectant, sincere, brimful of believing
and every morning she crawls back to her garden,
untangles her bent wings, sticks her head in the birdbath.
Her lovers always insist on coming down.
The bright eyes, last night, that stared right at her,
become staid, serious, look right through her.
Sometimes they're not drunk. Sometimes they're crazy.
She gets treated like a symptom.
They take blinding pills and stop returning calls.
The fairy likes the drunks, likes the crazies,
she's aroused by the feverish – those hot and brief affairs,
but the lonely, fuck, they really kill her,
with their coffee and their realism
and their 'not coming out to play.'
When she masturbates – and fairies often do –
she dreams of tired skin, dry lips,
she dreams of losing herself on worn carpets,
stained fingers, the sad and suffocating love
of the lonely. The fairy is bored with her garden,
bored with her windchimes, her lip-gloss,
her tiny shiny singing voice.
She wants someone who doesn't need enticing,

who finds her somewhat dull and ordinary,
who picks her sequins off the pillow with disdain,
drapes her with a heavy arm. She wants snores
that rip the darkness, darkness that leaves in the morning,
ripe, huge bodies that remain. The fairy wants
to groan, to fart, to stay for breakfast.
The fairy wants to be ripe and huge.

TROUBLE CAME TO THE TURNIP

When trouble came to the village
I put my love in the cabbage-cart
and we rode, wrapped in cabbage,
to the capital.

When trouble came to the capital
I put my love in the sewage pipe
and we swam, wrapped in sewage,
to the sea.

When trouble came to the sea
I put my love inside a fish
and we flitted, wrapped in fish,
to the island.

When trouble came to the island
I put my love on a pirate ship
and we squirmed, wrapped in pirate,
to the nunnery.

When trouble came to the nunnery
I put my love inside a prayer book
and we repented, wrapped in prayer,
to the prison.

When trouble came to the prison
I put my love on a spoon
and we balanced, wrapped in mirror,
to the soup.

When trouble came to the soup
I put my love inside a stranger
and we gritted, wrapped in a mouth
to the madhouse.

When trouble came to the madhouse
I put my love on a feather
and we flapped, wrapped in feather,
to the fair.

When trouble came to the fair
I put my love inside a rat
and we plagued, wrapped in rat,
to the village.

When trouble came to the village
I put my love in the turnip-lorry
and we sneaked, wrapped in turnip,
a hurried kiss.

FROM 'WATERING CAN' (2009)

ROAD-SIGNS

You were travelling a grey motorway.
You had a baby in your lap
with enormous green eyes
and a scarily large head.
You parked the car in a lay-by, sat on the roof,
held her high like a trophy,
joked, 'One day all of this will be yours.'

Then you crunched the leaves from the trees
into a mess of green and said, 'These are leaves.'
Baby said, 'Show me something else.'
You showed your baby the ocean
and baby said, 'Salty.'
You showed your baby mud
and baby covered herself in mud.
You showed your baby a grown man
and baby said, 'Let's give some green
to that man and some ocean and some mud.'
So you did. Then you showed your baby tears
and baby said, 'Ocean?'
Then you showed your baby blood
and baby said, 'Salty,'
and you said, 'Don't drink that,'
and baby said, 'Muddy man,
and baby said, 'Bloody leaves,'
and baby said, 'The ocean is a green man with salty blood'
and you recognized your baby's madness.

Now I am a young woman
I travel the grey motorway alone
and women who are not my mother

teach me grey, acidic truths:
weather-girls trapped in thick glass buildings,
situation comedies with boldly coloured sofas,
mini-markets flourishing in meteorite craters.
I pop the cork on my strange vinegar bottle,
try to become unrecognisable.

But when I return,
the swaddling-wraps still steaming on the floor
from when I evaporated, my mother
pours green tea, shows me the tyre marks on her wrist –
souvenirs from the grey motorway.
Then she points at the sky and says,
'Those are clouds,'
then she takes me outside and says,
'This is sunlight'
then she pushes me down a well and says,
'That is darkness'
and I mean to say, 'Obviously'
but I say, 'Bandages, griddle and ouch'
I say, 'Griddle my bandages'
I say, 'Sunlight my ouch'
I say, 'Bandaged clouds griddle darkness with sun'
and I run inside to find a pen
and my mother shouts, 'A is for Apple!'
and I write and I write and I write
our sweet green poem.

FAMILIAR GROUND

Red Riding Hood went back to the spot
where she was nearly mauled
and she waited.

A hairy man in a hat
asked her for a cigarette.

She tilted down her sunglasses,
gave him a peek
of her bloody black eyes.

'Jesus Christ,' he said,
'What happened to you?'

'Rottweilers, bears, gorillas,' she said,
'Lions, tigers…pigeons even,
they've all taken a shot.
By the way, sonny, I know who *you* are.'

'You've changed,' he said, 'you're sharper,
wiser, I can see that.'

Then he offered her a bottle
and she drank like an outlaw
until her eyes rolled back in her head.

The wolf dragged her body to a clearing
and they were not separated.

When dawn broke, she regained consciousness.

The wolf was leaning by an oak, looking sweaty.
It had been too easy.

Red Riding Hood smiled a cough
and wiped her mouth.
'I must have nodded off,' she said,
'I didn't do anything daft last night did I?'

'No,' said the wolf, 'you were charming.'

'Oh good,' she said
and staggered off through the trees,
her dress tucked into her tights.

LAST TUESDAY

I miss my Tuesday so much. I had a Tuesday
today. But it wasn't the same. It tasted funny.
There were signs it had already been opened.
The seal was broken. Someone had poisoned it
with Wednesday-juice. In fact, I think today
was actually Wednesday but the government
was trying to pass it off as Tuesday by putting
my tennis lesson back a day, rearranging the
tea-towels. I sent a letter to MI5 and the CIA
and the rest. I know they have my Tuesday.
They're keeping it for experiments because it
was so freakishly happy. I was smiling in my
sleep when two men in body-sized black socks
stole it from my bedside table. It was here.
It was right here. But when I woke up, it was
gone. Their Wednesday stole my Tuesday.
Their frigging totalitarian cloud-humped shit-
swallower of a Wednesday stole my innocent
Tuesday. And now it's just getting ridiculous:
the days change every week, it's like an avalanche.
As soon as I start to get the hang of a day, learn
the corridors, find my locker-key, the bell goes
and suddenly it's Thursday, or Friday, but not
last Friday or Thursday, oh no, these are different
ones, with knee-caps like pustules, gangly eyes,
you never know which way they'll lunge.

In the Lost Property Office, I held up the queue.
It's greenish, I told the attendant, with a mouth
that opens to a courtyard. But they only had a box
of wild Fridays some lads had misplaced in Thailand.
(I took a couple of those, for the pain.) Then I
gave up. I ignored the days and they ignored me.
I drank Red Bull in the ruins of monasteries,
flicking through calendars of digitally-enhanced dead
people: Gene Kelly downloading a remix
of 'Singing in the Rain' on his slimline Apple Mac.
No one gives a damn about time anymore. Happy hour
lasts all afternoon. You can put a hat on a corpse
and send it to work. You can bury a baby.

Hip counsellors in retro tweed jackets keep
telling me to look ahead. There'll be other Tuesdays
to enjoy, they say, new Tuesday pastures. It's a lie.
I found my Tuesday in someone else's bed.
Its chops were caked in velvet gel and its voice
had corrupted. It pretended to be a Saturday
but I could see myself reflected in its eyes, a younger
me, tooting the breeze with a plastic trombone.
'I'm sorry,' said my Tuesday, pulling its hand out
of a woman, 'I didn't mean to let you down but
I couldn't stay perfect forever, you were suffocating me.
Even sacred memories need to get their rocks off.'

WILD FLOWERS

I will be sober on my wedding day,
my eggs uncracked inside my creel,
my tongue sleeping in her tray.

I will lift my breast to pay
babies with their liquid meal,
I will be sober on my wedding day.

With my hands, I'll part the hay,
nest inside the golden reel,
my tongue sleeping in her tray.

I'll dance with cows and cloying grey,
spin my grassy roulette wheel,
I will be sober on my wedding day.

I'll crash to muddy knees and pray,
twist the sheets in tortured zeal,
my tongue sleeping in her tray.

Church bells shudder on the bay,
fingered winds impel the deal:
I will be sober on my wedding day,
my tongue sleeping in her tray.

PEAKED

Popped out,
showered off,
took my burden
down to the playschool,
bought a Lego mansion
they never finished building,
paid through the neck for twenty grams
of glitter glue, hit the chocolate milk,
learnt Danish with the purpose of reading
The Ugly Duckling in the original,
didn't see it through, washed-up, my fifth birthday bombed,
'I preferred your early work,' said a girl with measles,
'It was rawer, richer, these cupcakes seem hackneyed,'
superiors tried to placate me with kazoos,
plasticine crumbled to luminous ash,
my novelette about the hippo
was mistook for a comedy,
Miranda, that cunning bitch,
read her poem in class,
'My Doll,' it was called,
pretentious crap:
immature,
clunky.

DETOX

My sleepless one, I'm sending you green tea
across the timelines. Drink for a wellbeing effect.
I scraped the last grain of soil from my mouth,
been crashing a dodgem around the M1,
the newspapers are made of butter, folk
buttering their toast with stories of suicide
bombers dying from paper-cuts. Death
by eye contact. We're not allowed to look
at each other now, the army supplied us
with goggles. The air is too cold to breathe,
a man with an aerosol comes round once a week.
The bananas are straight like beanpoles
from the stress. The maps are wrong.
They found the leg of a car mechanic
under a car. The streets tinkle with light
jazz rain, the bus-shelters flicker like holograms,
one in ten people are invisible, I walked
through a woman on London Bridge;
I wouldn't have known but my clothes were silted
with spit and I felt like I'd just been ice skating.
My best friend got pregnant six times
in the last month, and already her kids
have left school and built their own parking lots
in the heart of New York. The life expectancy
of a fly is one second. The human brain is dirty
and infects the blood with 'Gongbellchimus,'
a contagious disease that causes the patient
to believe they have a large amount of gold
trapped inside their ribcage. Sometimes I feel
like one tiny lightbulb in a huge flashing poster
advertising peanuts. I've been avoiding food

with additives. Government officials in dentist chairs
wearing face-packs and reading philosophy.
Everyone is toned. Toned hair. Toned noses. Free
mineral juice. They're calling it 'The Grand Detox.'
I found a ring on the road which I put on my hand.

A LOVE SONG

Long before we tie the knot, Divorce moves in.
He sits on the naughty step, patting his knees.

Crowned in towel, I step out the shower
and he's there, handing me a raffle ticket.

He plays kickabout with the neighbourhood kids,
chalks crosses on their doors and buys them Big Macs.

Socking his fist into the bowl of his hat,
he'd kicked the gate wide, that sunny day in Leeds.

My mum was incredulous, 'She's only ten,
she can't possibly have made contact with you.'

He clocked my young face and handed me his card.
'Call me when you fall in love, I'm here to help.'

Perhaps he smelt something in my pheromones,
a cynicism rising from my milk teeth.

With gum, he stuck notes on Valentine's flowers:
tiny life-letters in factual grey ink.

The future cut two keys for a new couple.
On my twenty-first, Divorce took the spare room.

He loves to breathe down the spout of the kettle,
make our morning coffee taste mature and sad.

He waits by the car, slowly tapping Tic Tacs
down his throat. We've thought about stabbing him

but he's such a talented calligrapher:
our wedding invitations look posh as pearl.

He bought us this novelty fridge magnet set,
a naked doll with stick-on wedding dresses.

Divorce and I sometimes sit in the kitchen,
chucking odd magnetic outfits at the fridge.

He does the cooking, guarding over the soup,
dipping his ladle like a spectral butler.

He picks me daisies, makes me mix-tapes, whispers:
'Call me D.' Next thing he'll be lifting the veil.

After the honeymoon, we'll do up the loft,
give Divorce his own studio apartment.

We must keep him sweet, my fiancée agrees,
look him in the eye, subtly hide matches,

remember we've an arsonist in the house.
The neighbours think we're crazy, pampering him

like a treasured child, warming his freezing feet,
but we sing Divorce to sleep with long love songs.

THE MONOGAMY OPTICIAN

He held up laminated pictures of can-can dancers.
He drew a dot on the wall and said, 'Is it a foetus?'
He said, 'Hold your head back like you would at the hairdresser.'
He studied my retinas through a hole in a hammer.

He said, 'Unfaithfulness is a product of surplus sight,
it's the bridesmaid in the corner of the wedding photo.'
He said, 'Since my peripheries were surgically removed,
I've only had eyes for my wife. It's the miracle cure.'

He sent for his nurse in the living-mushroom apron.
She said, 'Your peripheries will be surgically removed.'
I said, 'Do you never sneak a glimpse on the underground?'
She caught my words in the gas mask like a baseball glove.

My grandparents had similar treatment in the fifties
though the peripheries were sliced by hand, before lasers.
Happy couples swooning the beach in their padded glasses,
colliding with bollards and donkeys and newsstands and deckchairs.

That night I flounced in: 'Honey, I went to the optician
and they fixed my wandering eyes, look I'll prove it.'
I dragged us to a sexy bar called The Kaleidoscope,
trained my gaze on your face like a sparrow in a neck brace.

When we split, I returned to the opticians in a sulk.
No cash refunds. The machines looked rusty in the daylight.
He said, 'It's not our fault if your peripheries grow back.'
I trudged home through the park with all the daffodils and... stuff.

CLOSET AFFAIR

When the shivers of shame have stopped, she said,
I'll just hop on a bus and go back to my husband
but first – this might sound odd – I want to sit
in your airing cupboard for a couple of hours.
The mortgage payments will be modest
and you have to knock if you want to come in
and I'll say, 'Who is it?'
and you'll say, 'I've brought you a cup of tea'
and I'll say, 'Leave it on the doorstep please, I'm in the shower.'
But, of course, I won't be.
I'll just be sitting there in the dark.

THE GOLDEN KIDS

She became an usher to an usher in an ushering firm
for failed burglars with tiny torches.

He had a baby by accident:
a blank colour house like a primary school foyer, hiding
from his baby, knees up in the Wendy house,
reading and re-reading the alcohol proverb.

She found happiness in love, of all places.

She fell for a millionaire
and locked herself in a house with cocaine
and playing cards and rung me occasionally
for stories of the city.

He became an astronomer without a telescope,
writing, 'Today will be a lucky day, but unlucky
things might happen,' bought a bong and settled down.

She walked in on a friend having sexual intercourse
with a dog and nothing was said except
'That's not your dog.'

She left the asylum to work in mental health care.
He left the rack to join the army.
She left the heroin to write a book.

He sat on the floor and waited for the surrealists
to convert his empty flat into an Indian elephant.

She bought a surfboard decorated with a painting
of the sunrise, propped it up like an ironing board
against the French windows and demanded it
make her carefree.

He became the thought of his wife in a bar with a man.

He became the thought of a man on a beach
at six in the morning with a broken metal detector.

He became the thought of a man on pills without pills
just going insane.

She became her own bearded Marilyn.

She went to build an orphanage on the other side of the planet
and left her goldfish behind. By goldfish, I mean children.

She had a school reunion: they wore their school jumpers,
they drank the old beer and blackcurrant and talked
about clinical depression as if it were a hip new motorcycle
they'd all invented together. *I've just bought the latest pillbox,*
such delicate workmanship, easy-open catch, a sturdy velvet base.
Steel grey is such a fashionable colour, don't you think?

He became a soft acoustic singer-songwriter and wrote
we've only got one life, my baby, so pass me the knife, my baby,
and I'll carve you a picture of my soft acoustic strife,
then floated off the stage to stick his soft acoustic penis in a groupie.

She became a state of the art homosexual
and silhouetted herself in tender smoke
with a book of women poets and a black and white film collection
of female erotica, and a defining haircut and a London apartment

with tapestries on the wall – woven by third world women –
and put a woman in her satin double bed and used the word vulva
in normal conversations and caught a plane to San Francisco
to parade the streets with a whistle around her neck,
wondering why the blue sky was so earnest
when all of nature's creatures united in tedium and she was still
so uncomfortable in cotton.

He became a state of the art heterosexual and cooked himself
strong dinners of fish and new potatoes, thinking
his arms would be so muscular if he was Australian.

She became the memory of six teenagers on a sweet tobacco sofa
in a crumbling house, saving their beer-caps, glad to be
contemplating suicide because the future is healing
the acne on their skin and they are the golden kids.

THIS POEM IS ACTUALLY ABOUT ME

Narcissus went to the pool.
Mothers were tossing boomerangs in the park,
fathers were catching them in their teeth.
Narcissus sat on the bank and hugged his knees, remembered
the kids he went to school with –
some had set up novelty jewellery shops
in the hollows of the Mediterranean,
some had turned into almond trees
or perished, snake-bitten and hoarse, whispering love songs.
He knew about the sleep of death,
when sweet music spoils inside your ear
and one night you call your dealer on the telephone,
ask for a storm to scatter your fleet.
Narcissus ran his fingers down his face, retraced
his ex-lovers:
beautiful birds with the heads of women
who stuffed their tail-feathers in his plughole, shrieking:
'You never listen, Narcissus, it's always about you!'
And the boys – dim, blank-looking boys
who marvelled their tongues along his jawline
then went back to class.
His ex-lovers were really not lovers at all.
Except one.

She arrived at the worst time,
he'd rented a hotel room,
started drinking the mini-bottles of conditioner,
anything to smooth his soul.
She had pinballed from commune to commune,
humiliating herself in karaoke bars

singing 'Mr Bojangles,'
and was looking for somewhere to bury her head.
Narcissus loved her, front way and back way,
with all the speed in his spluttering engine.
They staggered around, laughing, pretending
to be free. But this wasn't Paris. Paris isn't Paris.

He changed her name. He called her Echo.
It was funny at first.
'Echo! Make my dinner!'
'Narcissus! Make my dinner!'
But one minute they were touching hands
across the massive tablecloth, then
the candles torched the duvet, the bread rolls
jammed the toilet pipes, the forks
split their lips and the knives severed the rest.
And all he could say was 'you did this!'
And all she could say was 'you did this!'
They packed their bags simultaneously.
The last thing he needed
was someone exactly like him.

He got a job in a factory,
checking cabbages for worms,
checking his hands for liver spots.
He flew home to watch his mother die,
attached to a drip
in a very westernised hospital,
you could buy microwave hamburgers
from the vending machine…
a far cry from her sea-nymph days,
when she would drag men upstairs by the length of their ties
and Narcissus, a little boy, would hear
the roar of the ocean through the wall.

Now here he was, on this grassy verge,
by the oak tree
which once sported his tyre-swing.
Narcissus, a grown man,
with stretchmarks on his heart,
looking down into the pool
at his own face.
His eyes, clear blue and radiantly sad.
His skin, untouched by the wind
that rattled through his bones.
Narcissus splashed his lips against the water
and tried, he really tried,
to love himself.

FLATMATE

My shadow rolled up her loose, grimy sleeves,
slid off the stool where I was sipping juice,
picked my pocket with a hooked finger,
crept back with bagels and a bad habit.

My shadow stayed faithful until lunchtime,
watched GMTV upside down in bed,
clicked the wheel of her lighter and vanished.
The air span with stringy, puckered habits.

I'm not her mother. I can't stalk her
from streetlight to dustbin in muted shoes.
She ducked back through the cat-flap for dinner,
chewing on black wine-gums and her meek leer.

My shadow pressed a hot-water bottle
against my ruptured side and tucked me in.
Her mobile phone shivered like a habit.
A shred of stocking caught in the flung door.

My shadow dragged another shadow home,
their eyes dilated with rotten sunlight.
I slept under the bed with the secrets,
watching bed-springs flinch from their ghostly weight.

In the morning, I packed my clean notebooks,
my crisp underwear, my health magazines.
My shadow called me a fair-weather friend.
She scoffed, 'You want to live like a palm tree?

You want to walk with redheads on the beach,
drink milk with men in white suits and smugly
pride yourself on being ashamed of me?'
I fumbled the doorknob with my limp wrist.

Shadowless, the following years were a blur.
Blessings dissolved on my tongue like habits.
A degree, a smoke-free house, two bright kids,
a sundial in the backyard, chiming noon.

Hours before my death, I found my shadow
frozen-stiff on the swing-seat, skeletal.
Her feet were webbed from walking. Rejection
had fattened her habits, suckled her bones.

I offered up. Let her prepare my lids
with war-paint, shade my ribs with murmurs,
clip my door-keys to her belt. When night came
I lay beneath our cradle, cowering.

BOW YOUR HEAD AND CRY

When the ambulance finally rocked up,
its bouncy wheels rolling merrily over the cobbles,
our love was barely breathing.
I had been blowing into its mouth
but I must have blown too hard.
Our love had swallowed its tongue. The poor dear.
All the little old ladies, looking out from their teashops,
were muttering, 'What a shame'
and 'It was so young'.
Shut up, I said, and slapped one of them.
It's not dead yet. Look. Its legs are still moving.
Just then, its legs stopped moving.
The paramedics put on their duffel coats
because it had started to drizzle.
'Shall we get out the stretcher,' they asked,
'or would that be a bit pointless?'
I lay down beside our love
and held its teeny hand.
You weren't even there to witness the passing.

FROM 'THE HAT-STAND UNION' (2012)

POWERLESS

I was treated for fairy-godmother dependency.
I arrived with a crate of leaving presents:

A cling-film sculpture of fog from Mother Urge,

a permanent-marker of smoke from Mother Longing,

a murmur in a Tupperware box from Mother Promise,

and five skinned prawns from Mother Hope
(in case I got peckish for a bite of almost nothing.)

The first thing my healers did
was confiscate my hamper.

They sat me with a group of human protégées.
Their skulls like mine bore florescent scars
from the tap-tap-tap of magic wands.

Mother Numb made the best aspartame cheesecake.
Carcinogenic, it tasted like heaven.

'Is there sweet-and-low for my coffee?' I asked,
'I just need a pinch of sweet-and-low.'

'We came into these rooms,
broken by desire…' said the speaker,
pale behind a black lectern.

His facial skin was slack
with protruding beige teeth marks, like his brain
had grown a mouth and started chewing its way out.

'Can I please have some fucking sweetener for my shit coffee?'
I asked again.

They spoke of hands briefly leafing through their hair,
a kiss on the cheek that might have been the wind.
'These are our honeyed moments,' they said,
'And they are not enough to live on.
They are not enough to keep us sane.'

THE DRY WELL

In the dry light of morning, I return to the well.
You think you know the outcome of this story.

Sunshine is a naked, roaming thing like hurt.
A well is a chance embedded in the ground.

The well was dry yesterday and the day before.
You think you know the lot about sunshine –

an early bird knows sod all about perseverance.
Good people, you lay down your curling souls

on the dust and surrender. I swing my bucket.
If the well is dry today I will come back tomorrow.

HOW THE WILD HORSE STOPPED ME

I was punching in the last digit of your number
when a wild horse came up to me and said,
'Would you agree gathering information is an important way
to help people make decisions?' 'I guess,' I said.

'So you'd agree surveys can help decide
where money should be spent, what products to purchase,
what problems there might be in the near and/or distant future?'
'Uh huh.' I tried again to dial.

'And your ideal survey...would it have A) Big questions B) Small
        questions. C) Stupid questions. D) Impossible questions?'
'I haven't time for this.'
The horse snorted in the manner of his species,
'I'll put you down for E) I just want silence in my head.'

'I. Am. Calling. My. Date. OKAY?'

The wild horse shook his dark mane. Stood aghast.
He gave a thespian whinny.

'Write your favourite colour on this scrap of paper then drop it
in the fish bowl. Thanks. Now pick one from the bowl.'
'There's only mine in there.' 'Let's see! Let's see!'
'Purple.'
'We only accept primary colours. I'll tick blue and red....

Do you ever go down to the river?
A) Not since mother/father/sister/brother/everyone went mental.
B) Not since I fell in love.

C) Not since I pretended to move on.
D) My face is wet with river water. I have a watermark across my chin.'

'B. No. C. No. C. No. C.'

'Which of the following questions could be described as 'open ended?
1) Did you think I couldn't tell your eyes wrote patterns of yearning on
    my chest?
2) Is there a second hand on this watch?
3) Has nature ever been violent towards you when intoxicated?
4) Will you marry me – just once – before I die?'

The horse was not a normal horse.
He had a look, like a sexual predator.
Three months had passed and I hadn't called you.
You had found somebody else or starved to death by the phone.

The wild horse was sobbing and soliloquizing.
'Do you realize what I've sacrificed for your pointless survey?' I
    shouted.
'What survey? I'm a horse.'

DAY ROOM

Some crazy people believe they are Napoleon.
I am Alexander I of Russia, enthralled by Napoleon.
I declared, somewhat tardily, 'We can no longer reign together!'
after my small friend invaded me in 1812.

You think I'm joking.
Lip-chewing Meg is deluded about being Napoleon
but I *am* Alexander I of Russia, betrayed, muddled, conflicted.

This is not a metaphor. From my football coach
I learnt Rousseau's gospel of humanity, from my babysitter
I learnt the traditions of Russian autocracy and when I said

'The limits of liberty are the principles of order,'
what I really meant to say was:
I give up.

I'm taking my dying empress for a change of air.

THE ISLAND WOMAN OF COMA DAWN

My feet dart in the water
like sad guitarist fingers.
I've come here to carve.

Such calm mineral caves.
Tomorrow Trojan ducks
will bob, quack in beeps.

I'm ridden from all love,
distilled in exiled pause,
weightless soul-case, free.

Sunrise in Coma Dawn is
a timid rising in the air,
eyelash chance of a kiss.

Then one breath of light
reborn up yesterday's pipes
stubs answers on my eye.

Jungle of parasols hears no
snores, no nosy footfalls. I can
defecate in orange groves.

DAMAGE

Her teddy bear eloped with her mother.
Her father went to buy flowers for himself
on Father's Day and never came home. Her grandma
was a wastepaper basket. She was raised by staplers.
Her skin was deathly white. Her birthmark
was the shape of Africa. No one explained
anything to her. She excelled at school until
she was abused by her own calculator. She ran
away from home to join a troupe of travelling
accountants. She could balance a Filofax on her head
and yawn at the same time. Audiences loved her.
She married a man called Jerry, who turned out to be
a hat-stand in disguise. She contracted a disease
transmitted by celibacy. She slept in a violin case, smoking
rosin. She lost all pleasurable sensation in her ears.
She drank to forget. She drank to remember where
she'd left her bike. You met her during the winter.
She said, 'I need someone to save me.' You did
what any sensible person would have done.

THERE ONCE WAS A BOY NAMED BOSH

There once was a boy named Bosh
who had a Shallow family. Daddy
Shallow dealt in motorcars, his favourite
word was 'repercussion' and he always
kept Mummy Shallow in pocket if not
in peace. She was a narcissist who'd
perfected the wilting flower. Doctor
Shallow gave her pills for her nerves.
'We all have nerves,' said Bosh, but
Brother Shallow was found hanging
in the attic like an off lightbulb so
Grandma Shallow did the cooking
and Shallow neighbours constructed carpools
to get Bosh to school. Teacher Shallow
collected money for nearly-dead children
in hot places and Bosh was supposed to
say a little something in assembly but
Brother Shallow was all-the-way dead
and where's his money? The Shallow girls
found Bosh mean and sexy when he got
blind with self-loathing. Mummy Shallow
said, 'Why can't you play football?' because
she only cared about external achievements
and Daddy Shallow polished himself in his
dark Mercedes. 'It's like they are zombies,'
Bosh thought, 'Who don't have any blood:
eating their McDonald's onion rings, telling
me they're hurting too,' so Bosh started
drinking lots and lots of beer and whisky
like an adult does when he loses something
big like a poker game or a piece of paper

with a number on it. 'My Shallow family
are so Shallow,' Bosh said, 'they probably
wouldn't notice if I was hung too' and
Bosh was wrong about this, but Bosh put
a dressing gown cord round his neck as
Daddy Shallow watched *American Beauty*
downstairs and Sister Shallow swallowed
leeches in her bedroom to get skinny and
Mummy Shallow wrote in her pink leather diary.

FANTASY ROLEPLAY

You had two children. They were present, like crickets,
too young to do anything but lie there and feel.
Your husband was a reactive blink to an inappropriate comment.
Your house was the shape of a lucky horseshoe.
There were archways and guard dogs and roses. 'I love you,' I said
as you closed the door, screamed, opened it again then silently
packed little Lionel and Greta into my car, stuffed your satchel
with apples from the tree you were married under
and got into the passenger seat.

We listened to 'Dig A Pony' by The Beatles
and sang, 'She can penetrate any place she goes!'
while the kids played rock-paper-scissors in the back.
You wouldn't let me kiss you for the first two weeks.
I had to wear a plastic Spider-Man mask.

One day, we were sitting in the Black Magic bar
of the Dawdle Bug hotel, wondering how to get
Lionel and Greta into private school. You looked so beautiful
drinking a pint of soda water with your big gloves on.
I said, 'Do you regret dropping your husband like that?
Leaving your perfect life? Sleeping on the road?'

'My name is Marcella,' you said,
I worked as a maid in the Jefferson's household.
The woman you loved was a cold and passive mother
and her husband was needy, disloyal
and collapsible. They were always fighting,
throwing plates, cleaning products, fridges

at each other, mushing Lionel's face into his broccoli,
shunting Greta around like a mini vacuum cleaner.
When you arrived, I saw the chance to give them a better life.'

'Do you really think I can give you a better life?' I said.
'Look,' said Marcella the maid, 'Lionel and Greta
are so peaceful around us now.
Lionel's like a tiny philosophy professor
and Greta's shadow puppets have a Rothko soul.
We're like the parents they were always meant to have.'

'I love you so much,' I said.
'I'm still very angry with you, Mr Jefferson,' you said.
'I know,' I said, breathing softly through my nose
as the sun came up on the Black Magic bar
and our battered faces. You bit into an apple.
'My name is not Mr Jefferson,' I said,
'I am their gardener, Alejandro.
Let's wake up the children and go home.'

SPAT

'It's me or the dog,' she laughed,
though by 'dog' she meant 'void'
and by 'laughed' I mean 'sobbed'
and by 'me' she meant 'us'
and by 'she' I mean 'you'
and by 'or' she meant 'and.'
'It's us and the void,' you sobbed.

A DIALOGUE BETWEEN ARTIST AND MUSE

JOHN DONNE: A fly is a more noble creature than the sunne, because a fly hath life and the sunne hath not.

A FLY: I find you extremely patronising.

KISSING

Like two teardrops racing down opposite faces
of the same hypocrite, their separate fabrications
form a single pool of clothes.

They are kissing to share the blame.
They are kissing to confuse their dental records.

If not tomorrow,
one of them must wake to be the one
unpicking from the plan, sliding out
from the tower of anniversary cards

onto the flat road. They are kissing to delay
the string of paper dolls asking to be real boys
and real girls. They are sucking the sting
from the lips that someday
will blurt

and, like surfacing from a cinema in mid afternoon,
will meet the daylight scandalised.

RUN

If my language was water
it would be rainwater

no-flow in bucket, gutter,
brow, no-flow in dust,

liquid thunder crumbed
in clay, sludge afraid

to slip away, since clouds
spewed out secrets,

water-babies sent like slop,
like lava, fevered blood.

At night, downstream culverts
bundle their passage

back underneath a train,
a road, a city wall:

can't you hear the sound
of that old drowning song?

If the bedrock sings along:
job's a good 'un

but drainage systems spin
in dreams and bits resurface like

'percolate,' 'swale', 'dinghy',
'sloop'; surf boards glitter

with buzz words, beaches
blotted in lisps of 'luff'

under a speaking moon:
'I dream to keep you yet

cursed to neap you! Alas,
but my hands are tides.'

She laps me, gulp, laps me
not. If my silence was water

I'd be heading for you, top
news bulletin, forecast

world over: babe grab a
coat, zip up, storm's coming.

MYSTERY TEARS

You could order them from China over the Internet.
The website showed a grainy picture of Vivien Leigh
in *Streetcar Named Desire*.
It was two vials for twenty euros
and they were packaged like AA batteries.

They first became popular on the young German art scene –
thin boys would tap a few drops into their eyes then
paint their girlfriends, legs akimbo and faces cramped
with wisdom in the style of the Weimar Republic. It was
sexy. They weren't like artificial Hollywood tears,
they had a sticky, salty texture
and a staggered release system. One minute,
you're sitting at the dinner table eating a perfectly nice steak
then you're crying until you're sick in a plant pot.

My partner sadly became addicted to Mystery Tears.
A thousand pounds went in a month
and everything I did provoked despair.
She loved the trickling sensation.
'It's so romantic,' she said, 'and yet I feel nothing.'
She started labelling her stash with names like
For Another and *Things I Dare Not Tell*.
She alternated vials, sometimes
cried all night.

She had bottles sent by special delivery marked
Not Enough. A dealer sold her stuff cut with
Fairy Liquid, street-name: *River of Sorrow*.

Our flat shook and dampened. I never
touched it. Each day she woke up

calmer and calmer.

A DISGRUNTLED KNIGHT

My armour is not polished: I am not a poster boy.
I make the ugly red-brown stains on the battlefield.
The celebrity knights only stay for the fanfare
then make a big show of leaving purposefully –
'What's that you say? Knights with blow-dried hair
needed urgently for an Easter Egg hunt? Come on boys!'
Some have ten year contracts as romantic leads,
can't lose a fingernail let alone a leg. Later they'll
canter back to the castle cheering, waving a flag
and our people will sleep tight as Camelot falls.

This is pretend war. I feel pretend hate. Unicorn!
Unicorn! My kingdom for a unicorn!
Someone still has to stay here and die.

FROM 'IN THESE DAYS OF PROHIBITION' (2017)

A SURREAL JOKE

One year is blank on my curriculum vitae.
I was in the desert, convalescing,
repairing my septum. I'd tried to die
expensively, dragging it out over
six months, locked in my university
bathroom with a rolled-up scrap of canto.
I forgot how to love my family.
At one point, my arms turned completely blue.

My assigned counsellor told me I used
poetry to hide from myself, unhook
the ballast from my life; a floating ruse
of surreal jokes. He stole my notebook.
I said, they're not jokes. He said, maybe try
to write the simple truth? I said, why?

PATIENT INTAKE QUESTIONNAIRE

Do you taste pepper whilst eating ice cream?

Do sandwiches appear intricately designed?

Do you think of waterfalls when lighting a match?

Have you started to look at pigeons like they know something?

Do you think about your chin when you are kissing?

Can you feel the blood in your thumb?

Do your eyebrows feel like stickers?

Do you look twice at your name on a letter?

Does your hair hurt?

When barefoot, do your shoes feel too tight?

Can you sense the tiny holes in the cotton of your shirt?

Do you peel bananas fearfully in case there is no banana inside?

Does the ceiling occasionally ripple?

Has your pillow developed a strange echo?

Does your neck feel like a bone?

Do you hear sex noises through the wall when standing in a field?

STEPHANIE

She was eighteen, used 'party' as a verb, lashes
like the whiskers of an oil-soaked seal, devoured
books with names like 'Steamy LA nights' under
the duvet by flashlight. I was twenty-three, brooding
over John Ashbery between therapy sessions, hunched

at the smokers table like a misunderstood genius.
I was recovering from a bout of 'goodbye world.'
We were both diligent pleasers. I fell in love
with the reflection of someone charming in her
sunglasses. I always wanted to be charming.

I forgot we were ill. When I finally touched her,
her skin dilated, she shuddered, licked her teeth
and crawled towards me across the bed. It was like
watching a child possessed by the vengeful spirit of a
murdered porn star. I locked myself in the bathroom

and then strode to the nurse's station to 'confess.'
Afterwards, my counsellor said
'We really dropped the ball on this one,
placing a sex-addict in a room with a lesbian.'
It'd never occurred to them.

She wrote me a ten-page love letter in red ink.
The nurses tried to lull my guilt: 'If an alcoholic
screams for a whiskey, it's not the bartender's fault
if he pours.' I didn't like being compared to booze,
like I could've been anyone – that acne-scarred chef

who grinned at her once, the mouthy car-washer
at the NA meeting, the pin-eyed new boy – like it was
just because I was her roomie and she was a nympho
and nothing to do with real electricity or Stephanie
somehow spying the part worth saving in me.

THE RAGS

When love comes through
the vents, you press wet rags against
the grill, lest you are smoked out
of your loneliness; you tape egg boxes
to your ears so you can't hear
the hissing; you swathe yourself
in shame like vinegar
and brown paper. At sundown,
you gather up the rags
and press them to your face
like the dress of a lover, hoping for
a slight effect, the remnants of a rush –
not enough to change your mind – just
enough to pacify the night.

The more beautiful women who gather around my bed
with their soapy smells and letter-writing hands,
the more deeply I pretend to be locked in this coma.

They link arms in a circle, sing hymns, swapping
the Oh Lord bits for my name. Most are singing ironically
but one or two are terrifyingly serious. At dusk,

the eldest of the serious ones creeps in the window
to sit and stroke my ankle with a feather. It's unnerving,
I don't enjoy it. Occasionally she whispers, 'I know' –

but I think she's just responding out loud to demanding
late-night work emails. Once, she pressed a big hard book
against my brow. *That had better not be the Bible,*

I thought. Obviously I couldn't say anything. 'Casanova
in Coma' is the role of a lifetime. You can't corpse.
If I'm feeling reckless, I might lift my lids for a second

when the room is empty and still, just to reassure myself
I'm not dead. But that's it. I can't risk one of the beautiful
women catching me with my eyes open. The nurses

march in to change my dirty tubes in funereal silence
like I'm already an object, spiritless, personality-free.
I prefer their brisk touch, it asks for little. Hell,

it doesn't even ask me to live. *Poor woman,* I hear them
think, but this means nothing. They think *Poor woman*
about everyone including household pets and men.

I'm baffled by the amount of edible goods I've received.
Last time I chanced an eye-flutter, my room resembled
an artisan food market loaded with quince, baklava,

ostrich burgers, hand-crafted chocolates in trendy boxes.
Who is it all for? They'll be bringing me kites next,
pogo sticks, bmxs. They've forgotten what a coma entails,

it's like they're preparing for some almighty comeback,
a sudden Lazarus moment when I leap from the linen,
devour twenty truffles in one gulp, passionately snog

all of them, in turn, with my stale tongue, then ride out
the corridor on a gift-wrapped skateboard as they run
behind, whooping, throwing grapes like confetti.

That is their communal dream. But then what? We all
live in a house together? I choose one? Choose none?
And the gratitude, they'll expect so much. They'll say:

'I visited you every day in hospital, Casanova,
for three years. I even skipped my own mum's funeral
so as not to miss one twitch of your chiselled face...

and now you don't have time for a fucking latte?
Hello?!!' And they'll be correct. Of course. They'll be
so loudly spot-on and forthcoming with their love. I am

the most loved person in a pretend coma on this planet.
Tonight I plan to fake my own death.
I'll hold my breath for as long as it takes. Five hours

if necessary. Then, safe in the morgue, I'll unzip my body-bag, slip out into the spring evening. I'll fashion a mask out of big leaves. I'll head for the cluster of lights

on the mountain or wherever the music is coming from. Midges won't bite. Night-time will blank me. Barmaids, ignore me. I won't touch any skin that isn't mine.

TO BE EXPLICIT

I wanna rip you open
like a sack of doves,
press my skin to the stir
of hindered flight,
feel the flutter swell
into a wheeling room,
an exodus fathoming air
like a scream,
a strobe-lit punch, my
whole sky crammed
with your lost pressure;
pocket just one
souvenir feather and
leave you in peace.

My father was a hundred and five years old when he discovered the pleasures of crystal meth. At first I thought his gurning mouth and disjointed speech were symptoms of dementia. Imagine my relief when he slipped a baggie of white shards from the netted side-pocket of his Stannah Stairlift. He called it by its street-name, Tina. As he lit the glass pipe, he reminisced about a repressed Blackpool girl with the same name he'd courted gingerly after the war. 'Those days were clogged with woollen tights and shame,' he said, his pupils exploding behind his spectacles; 'Can you make me a website?' 'What?' I said, thinking I'd misheard. 'I want to advertise my wares,' he said. 'What wares?' I said. 'Bondage. Water Sports. Sadomasochism. People will pay good money to lick the toilet seat of a silver fox.' When he smiled his face lit up like an electrocuted skull. 'But you're a hundred and five years old...' He sunk in his sweater. '...Which is all the more reason', I added, 'not to waste another minute. Of course I'll make you a website. I'll even take the photos for you.' 'Will you paint my spare room dark, dark red?' he said. 'I'll buy the paint this afternoon,' I said. 'You're such a loving daughter,' he said, 'I've never felt so alive.'

He called himself The Pounding Pensioner. He was extremely popular. Women and men of all ages came and went at all hours of the day and night. The neighbours complained about the ecstatic howls. The Meals on Wheels bloke refused to enter the house, instead opting to leave the cloche of turkey mush and cauliflower cheese on the porch step. My father didn't mind. He didn't eat anyway. He wore his BDSM get-up twenty-four seven now: leather trousers, dog collar, studded platform boots. The kitchen lino was lacerated with whiplashes.

The last time I visited he was slow-dancing to trance music in the hallway with a young bodybuilder. They were both naked. 'Dad,' I shouted, 'Dad! I've brought you the *Radio Times* and that John le Carré audiobook you asked for!' No response. Embracing, they resembled one mannequin sporting a creased shawl of skin. His hearing aid was curled up in the condom bowl like an elf's liver. 'Dad!' I watched for a minute then let myself out. He wasn't coming down again. Not for anyone. He was with the angels now.

THE FEAR

Every day I picture you dead.
Splayed between two traffic cones,
unresponsive. Punched into prayer
beneath a windscreen's cracked sky.
Face down in a puddle of yourself.
If you're two minutes late, I sense
police on the porch,
                    their loaded lips.

We are the laughing lovers
in the reconstruction, just
moments before the attack.
The happy times. Pre-crash.

Last night, in bed, your arms
hurt like a jolted seatbelt.

PUBLIC RESOURCE

There is a place called The Open
where brave people put things.
Things that belong to them.
Things they can no longer carry.
Big things. Or little things
they fear are growing. All
those private rainbows
watered in pot-plants on dark
windowsills that suddenly
sprang up overnight
into twisting rollercoasters
tonguing through your flat… Things
that have become a *thing*.

It's like fly-tipping but legal
and you don't need a truck.
There's no limit to the amount
one person can offload. No
toxicity regulations. The Open
can swallow it. It is always
hungry. There will be no rising
smoke, after-odour, no bell-ringer
in a tower grabbing a rope, no
consequence unless
you dive in with it.

Can I shoot you entirely in standard definition digital video?
Can I shoot you right up in your gob like this?
Can I shoot you soot-faced and scandalised and laughing on the other
side of the street? Can I shoot you in my trailer with a pet monkey?
Can I shoot you with ketchup on your tights?
Can I shoot you hiccupping in the blood-rain?
Can I shoot you reaching for a metal doorknob?
Can I shoot you running without shoes? Can I
shoot you writhing on a lime green and black carpet, screaming
'Look at me!'? Can I shoot you fading in and out?
Can I shoot you suffocating inside a harp case?
Can I shoot you sliding into obscurity?
Can I shoot you shooting up? Can I shoot you shooting yourself?
Can I shoot you shooting out the barrel of a water slide at Fun World?
Can I shoot you on your knees looking up at me with forgiveness?
Can I shoot you on a plinth looking down at me with gratitude?
Can I shoot you on your back like a helpless tortoise?
Can I shoot you gazing directly into my lens reciting wedding vows?
Can I shoot you with a gear-stick for a leg?
Can I shoot you pointing at a gravestone with a crimson leather glove?
Can I shoot you with the whores of Warsaw, doing the locomotion?
Can I shoot you after midnight crawling out of a box with a burnt crack-
pipe mouth? Can I shoot you sweeping the porch of a wooden façade?
Can I shoot you walking down an alleyway with a bag of groceries
looking naïve and unsuspecting?
Can I shoot you every day for sixty-four years?
Can I shoot you witnessing the entire life of an orchid?
Can I shoot you raising twins, one mad and one sane?
Can I shoot you going through a messy divorce?
Can I shoot you with a rabbit's head on? Can I shoot you re-enacting

one scene from your childhood, unconvincingly? Please
let me shoot you in a nameless city deluged by continuous rain. Please
let me shoot you while you slowly disappear down a crack in Hollywood
boulevard. I so want to shoot you succumbing to a gypsy curse.
You think I haven't shot a lady right up in her vaginal wall before?
You think I haven't shot an addled hooker with a nightmarish clown face
sitting on a molten chair in the shape of a slumped obese man?
Can I shoot you so close your eyeball-jelly glistens? Can I shoot you
making love to a memory? Can I shoot you until I forget my own life?
Can I shoot you on a murdered girl's camera?

I saw hands reaching out of the bookcases.
I saw the bookcases stretching out of themselves.
I saw a man sitting on the end of the bed.
I saw wolves in the wardrobe.
You tried turning on the lights.
You tried splashing me with water.
You sat me on the sofa with a mug of tea.
I said, 'We all need to journey into a pit.'
Children were staging a play at the end
of the bed. You said, 'Baby, are you telling
me a story?' I said, 'This is *my* story.'
You called 999. I dribbled out my tea.
You said, 'My girlfriend's making no sense.'
I told the paramedics I was twenty-five.
I couldn't remember how to walk.
They were in my living room shining
torches, discussing my pupils.
I was lightly inhabited like a vapour.
I told the neon woman I lived on 'Address Road'.
I got my postcode wrong. And my birthday.
I couldn't remember my mum's maiden name.
I said Queen Elizabeth the First was on the throne.
When asked my dad's name, I listed Alan, Tom, Richard,
Mark, Sam, Luke, William, Graham, Martin, Harry...
In the ambulance I turned to you and said,
'Don't worry baby, I've got this.'

THE MILITARY LIFE OF A MAVERICK TEARDROP

Venturing out, unchartered skin, the moon-face
of a cheek, the precipice of a chin, our very own
Captain Oates in the tear-duct tent: 'I am just
going outside. I may be some time.'

Yes, Solitary Tear, we thank you for your service.
Individualist. Luminary. Brief Candle. Our Saline
Saint of Acceptable Sorrow. For years you hid us
from the world's horrors. Sleeves. Tissue boxes.

Snot. Shame. You held us back for our protection,
Solitary Tear, and now we must respectfully beg
you relinquish that role, Sir, and rejoin our ranks
because the sobbing situation's crazy out there

in the bedroom, study, lounge, it shows no sign
of resolution, all night long we hear fresh tears
screaming in squashed slang, sliding, colliding;
they do not wait their turn for the dive anymore,

spill out ten at once, some must shed and splat
never even knowing what it was they wept for.
This is no longer a job for an embroidered hanky,
Comrades. The time has come for us all to shine.

48 VENEER AVENUE

Imagine a hologram fire. Paper
angels stuck to fake-frosted windows.
Snow-sugared roof. A creaking
weathervane featured in the film score
(epiphany motif, like a harpist's trill).
Picture a broad porch, generic
actor coming home for Christmas
with a necessary speech, shiny
tower of gifts balanced under
his lantern chin. That is my house

as seen from the street. Behind
the front, where I live, it's mainly
scaffolding, audio equipment.
I sit cross-legged in the sawdust,
clutching a mic: 'Daddy's home,
Mummy!' My domain is domestic
sound effects, ghosts of the throat,
sweet impressions. On clear days still
I imagine you'll come knocking
at my 'door' to meet me in person.

Hey! I've got a theme song in my tooth,
Tabasco spleen, a reason to say 'halcyon',
a cobbler on speed-dial who specialises in
stretchy glass slippers, an honorary degree
from the Hot Pink Sensorium, two tickets
for literally every aeroplane, all laid atop
the chiffon in my valise but right now I'm
thinking about moonstruck linen, beaded
skin, a lover swallowed by my sighing or
maybe I'm planning a heist, it's hard to tell
with my hood up and sunglasses, shivering
in sweatpants etc but I am a neon fish, an
interstellar anomaly, undercover angel sent
to test you, yes please do admire the greasy
knots in my hair like precious gems dipped
in chip fat or perspiring padlocks – or these
dirt-smeared stars dangling above me, look,
that my Limbo Support Team say I have to
polish back to shining brilliance using only
a j-cloth and 'cleansing teardrops from my
congruent mind' before I ascend any higher.

MEGAN MARRIED HERSELF

She arrived at the country mansion in a silver limousine.
She'd sent out invitations and everything:
her name written twice with '&' in the middle,
the calligraphy of coupling.
She strode down the aisle to 'At Last' by Etta James,
faced the celebrant like a keen soldier reporting for duty,
her voice shaky yet sure. I do. I do.
'You may now kiss the mirror.' Applause. Confetti.
Every single one of the hundred and forty guests
deemed the service 'unimprovable.'
Especially the vows. So 'from the heart.'
Her wedding gown was ivory; pointedly off-white,
'After all, we've shared a bed for thirty-two years,'
she quipped in her first speech,
'I'm hardly virginal if you know what I mean.'
(No one knew exactly what she meant.)
Not a soul questioned their devotion.
You only had to look at them. Hand cupped in hand.
Smiling out of the same eyes. You could sense
their secret language, bone-deep, blended blood.
Toasts were frequent, tearful. One guest
eyed his wife — hovering harmlessly at the bar — and
imagined what his life might've been if
he'd responded, years ago, to that offer in his head:
'I'm the only one who will ever truly understand you.
Marry me, Derek. I love you. Marry me.'
At the time, he hadn't taken his proposal seriously.
He recharged his champagne flute, watched
the newlywed cut her five-tiered cake, both hands
on the knife. 'Is it too late for us to try?' Derek whispered
to no one, as the bride glided herself onto the dance floor,
taking turns first to lead then follow.

A TODDLER CREATES THUNDER BY DANCING ON A MANHOLE

At first, she cannot account for the noise.
With each jerked step, a thunderclap.
Her metal dance floor echoes her jive.
Her pumps, no bigger than mini croissants,
each create a cymbal crash, the earth
responds to her slightest step. What dark
sorcery is this? What topsy-turvy witchcraft?
She pauses to evaluate. A scientific test.
She retreats to the grass, jumps. No thunder.
She steps back on the manhole. Thunder.
She sees her powers are site-specific,
unique to this one patch. She returns
to her sacred sphere, a pint-size Jedi
embracing the force. I watch it happen
in her face. From this beer-garden bench,
book propped, ornamental, in my hands,
I see her eyes spin like stop-signs, red
to green. Now she cannot be silenced.
Prospero in rainbow leggings. Storm Lord.
She gambols fitfully on her audible stage.
(Toddlers always dance like marionettes,
their brains still learning the strings.) She
bellows with god-like glee. The men behind
are quaffing hipster ales: 'I don't want to
feel shit in terms of... there's never a good
way to end it...Daisy... I mean... she's fine.'
I turn my phone facedown on the table.
But what's this? A swerve in the plot?
A second child – same face, same rainbow
leggings – approaches the rim of the arena.
A sidelined gladiator. This is mythological:

siblings duelling for The Tempest Touch.
Yet in the magic circle is room for only one...
The twin hovers her trainer over the metal.
She pauses, draws back. I see her thinking:
What if I can't replicate the sound? Her logic
doesn't focus on the manhole, its looseness,
percussive material, the reasons for the noise,
but rather on her sister's ability to conjure it.
For the twin, it is not guaranteed *just anyone*
could make this dance floor sing, or that her
identical weight must yield identical magic.
The conclusion is unknown. Therefore, a risk.
A trial of self-belief. She lifts her foot again.
I miss my mouth, spill beer down my shirt.
Again, she withdraws. Her brow squeezes.
A moral flashes through it. And like that, she
folds, cross-legged, on the grass; consents to
spectate. She will not trespass on her sister's
fairy ring, steal her thunder. The humanity!
Generosity unsurpassed! Wait... there's more!
She begins to applaud, that fleshy infant clap
(its value enhanced by the coordinative strain).
The hipsters are discussing liquorice Rizla:
'It's flavoured smoking...' They chortle like
scrambled cassette tapes. But watch, now
the tiny dancer is a celebrity, applauded
by her own mirror image. An audience of
herself. Like that dream where everyone
looks like you. I pick up my phone, type
'I'm sorry' then delete it. I picture a world
of admiring clones, assigned doppelgängers
bred solely to approve of unremarkable feats;
a second Me sat cross-legged on my shadow,
shouting 'Bravo!' and 'It's a miracle! Look!
She can summon salty water from her eyes!'

THE AMNESTY

I surrender my weapons:
Catapult Tears, Raincloud Hat,
Lip Zip, Brittle Coat, Taut Teeth
in guarded rows. Pluck this plate
of armour from my ear, drop
it in the Amnesty Bin,
watch my sadness land among
the dark shapes of memory.

Unarmed, now see me saunter
past Ticking Baggage, Loaded
Questions, Gangs of Doubt; my love
equips me. I swear, ever
since your cheeky face span round
I trust this whole bloody world.

THE BLONDE AND THE ATOM AUTOMOBILE

Tonight I want to marvel at the woman
who ducks when she drives under bridges
as if her body is the car,
as if the top of her head is the sun roof,
as if she isn't in a car at all
just holding a steering wheel at arm's length
floating down the road, exposed,
motorway-wind in her bob,
no car seat either, squatting on space
like a lost figurine once glued
to a tiny bench on a train-set platform,
perched on the breeze, boot-tips
tapping air pedals, ringless hand
switching air gears, singing along to the radio
in her head – not connected to a satellite
but to space itself, where right now
the exploded remains of a supernova
roar like a billion invisible motors
soon to clump with other stardust
giving birth to a new self, brighter,
better than the one she used to be and
till that day comes she is just the whirling
bits of a heart blown open.
But look at her go. This blonde star in her car
made of atoms, revving on a wish,
brum   brum   brum...

FROM 'THE AIR YEAR' (2020)

PRIMITIVE HEART

You are the size of an orange seed and
developing a heart. Same, baby, same.
Your pre-heart is made of two tubes
which must fuse together now into one
primitive structure. Tell me about it.
By Friday your neural groove will herald
the beginning of your brain. Snap.
I'm a chickpea, bud, a tadpole,

pre-me. Within a week you'll double
in scope. I can't compete with that level
of personal growth. You'll outdo me, pip.
I'm unfused. Sketchy. Two heart strings
fumbling to combine. I'm not supposed to
dread completion, baby, am I? Yours nor mine.

THE GROUND

You land on a ridge, six-feet down the cliff
and believe you have fallen from the dread
summit and survived, you think,
this is the ground.
until you notice the larks passing at eye-level,
drop a cufflink and fall
fifty-feet into the open palm of another ridge,
deeper in, scratched, clothes torn,
you've lost a shoe but you think
this is the ground,
I can bake that lasagne now
till a kite gets snagged in your hair,
your feet meet a plunging carpet
now you're hanging by your necklace
from a branch thinking
this is the ground,
let's buy a puppy
as you sit in your bracken chair,
as you fall in your chair like a lopped flower head
face-planting – *Yes! Ground!* – in a tree,
wind-burnt from momentum, whip-
lashed by your own screams, oops, then oops,
oops, straddling a lamp-post, a pillar, a shed, each time
believing this is the ground, believing
you've survived, falling, landing, falling out,
who knows how long you've been travelling
down this thing, incrementally, held in the loosening-
tightening fist of a giant with a featureless face.
Thud. *At last*
I can put up that shelf. Make that baby.
You lie and let your bones heal, looking up

at the distance, experiencing plateau
for the first time, cold, hard, real, the opposite
of air. You shake like a prodigal astronaut.
I could build a house on this, you think,
staggering off.

SANITY

I do kind gestures. Remove my appendix.
I put my ear to a flat shell and – nothing.
I play the lottery ironically. Get married.
Have a smear test. I put my ear to the beak
of a dead bird – nothing. I grow wisdom
teeth. Jog. I pick up a toddler's telephone,
Hello? – No answer. I change a light bulb
on my own. Organise a large party. Hire
a clown. Attend a four day stone-walling
course. Have a baby. Stop eating Coco-Pops.
I put my ear right up to the slack and gaping
bonnet of a daffodil – . Get divorced. Floss.
Describe a younger person's music taste as
'just noise'. Enjoy perusing a garden centre.
Sit in a pub without drinking. I stand at the
lip of a pouting valley – SPEAK TO ME!
My echo plagiarises. I land a real love plus
two real cats. I never meet the talking bird
again. Or the yawning hole. The panther
of purple wisps who prowls inside the air.
I change nappies. Donate my eggs. Learn
a profound lesson about sacrifice. Brunch.
No singing floorboards. No vents leaking
scentless instructions. My mission is over.
The world has zipped up her second mouth.

DRAWN ONWARD

please love me
a little bit less, I'm standing on your front lawn yelling
for a helicopter, every morning the smell of your perfume gets
thicker, I mistook my heart
and urges for a twin set, the open road needs someone
like me, reversing through hedges
in my partner's world, plenty of others
hold tighter, if I had my own theme park I'd call it
Fuck It Monkey, I can't unzip this longing
in a service station toilet, strangle my
rising loss, I must stare down my face
in a coke-sugared mirror, spinning candy floss from
the breath of strangers, no images
compete with new ones, not enough oxygen in
old kisses
compete with new ones, not enough oxygen in
the breath of strangers, no images
in a coke-sugared mirror, spinning candy floss from
rising loss, I must stare down my face
in a service station toilet, strangle my
fuck it monkey. Can't unzip this longing?
Hold tighter. If I had my own theme park I'd call it
My Partner's World, plenty of others
like me, reversing through hedges
and urges for a twin set, the open road needs someone
thicker, I mistook my heart
for a helicopter, every morning the smell of your perfume gets
a little bit less, I'm standing on your front lawn yelling
please love me

THE DEADNESS

It's like being a windmill in a vacuum
packed village. Weekends are the worst.
The taste of nothing is like licking dew off plastic.
Floppy soul, they call it. Slack spirit. Neurological
pins and needles. Someone has drilled a hole in the crown
of my head, inserted a funnel, emptied
molten margarine into my plumbing. *Darling, are you listening?*
Did you know same-sex mice can procreate now?
You're already mid-anecdote about a colony of gannets
or a colleague's kidney stone removal. You're stomping
your wet boots, bashing white sprinkles from your hat
but the air hasn't moved in months, either
we're living in separate weathers
or you have fake snow on your coat.

NAPHTHALENE HEIGHTS

The hotel was called Naphthalene Heights
which I thought was a strange name for a hotel
but the poetry festival had booked me the room so I had no choice.

Besides, apart from the name, it was a completely normal hotel.

You were waiting for me in the lobby. You couldn't speak.

At the end of Alcestis by Euripides, Alcestis is brought back from
the underworld, mute. Her body has resurrected but her voice
remains dead.

'Is that what happened to you?'
You nodded. You still had soil in your hair.

'How did you die? Who killed you?'
We sat down in the bar. You ate a peanut and looked at me.

You were so beautiful I felt a commotion in the pit of my throat
like my words were fighting over you.

'Shall we order?'
There was a Fun Fact section under the children's menu
with colourful lettering inside speech bubbles rising from the mouth
of a cartoon snake.

*FUN FACT: In the past naphthalene was administered orally to kill
parasitic worms in livestock.*

It wasn't a cartoon snake, it was a cartoon worm.

FUN FACT: When you smell mothballs you are inhaling Naphthalene.

'Hotel food can be a little bland. We could eat somewhere else?'

You looked at me so sadly I felt continental plates separating
in my forehead. I studied the menu again.

*FUN FACT: Small children are at risk of eating mothballs, because they
look like candy or other treats.*

The food choices were standard.
Burgers, pies, ravioli. You pointed at a photo of a plate
of macaroni cheese then a photo of a glass of wine.
'Great.'

You coughed up a mothball.
It sat on the table between us like a sad, sucked imperial mint.

'Please say something.'
I handed you a pen.
'Write something on a napkin?'
It struck me that you were the death of the world.

I felt a terrible pain. I looked down.

A small hole was forming in my palm like a ghost was driving
a pencil through it.

'What's happening?'

You took my hand and stared at me through its hole.

Tiny holes were forming all over your face.
Pinpricks of light were shining out of you.
I realised 'holy' was a literal term. I didn't want to lose you
to the glare of the scene behind.

I could already see chairs and tables through you.
I could see the bar.
We were half-hotel.

I remembered that night you kissed me
in the car park of The Nobody Inn, you'd said
'In the next world maybe.'

We held our disappearing hands.

TEMPORARY VOWS

I hold two fingers to my head,
trigger my thumb, I say pow.
I slice my throat with a single stroke,
pull an invisible blade
vertically along my vein.
Remember the deaths we did together?
Twiddling oven knobs in the air
then thrusting our chins to inhale?
I loved you so much
during that experimental play
when you slowly leant forward to nick
your femoral artery then quietly
bled out in your seat until curtain call,
blood only we saw.
As well as death, we'd mime marriage.
I'd slide on a spectral ring
and you'd shiver at the thrill
of my thumb and fingertip
sealing the deal for a second till
the thought melted back into your skin.
I am proficient at beginnings,
The Air Year: the anniversary prior to paper
for which ephemeral gifts are traditional.
Only after our rings became solid
silver did they truly disappear.
Now the house is a mime scene.
Mime blood all over the floor,
trodden into carpet fibres,
shirts, bras, dried to an airy crust
under my nails. I slit
my neck at the traffic lights,

'pow' on the train, I suspend
my non-knife above my head,
'see what you're making me do.'
Red whirls rise from the cuts.
All these huge thoughts come to
nothing. My shadow is
the chalk outline of a woman
who did not jump.

The hovel belonging to The High Priestess of Love was even smaller and dirtier than I remembered. It looked like an igloo made from shit. The doormat was a slab of stone with 'welcome' scratched into it with a penknife. It is difficult to make a doormat sound sarcastic. As I stooped to enter, three giant wind chimes the size of trombones clattered stressfully above my head. A needlework sampler in the porch read 'Home is Where the Heart is so Where the Fuck is This?' The cuckoo clock ticked a hair too fast like a cocaine heartbeat. There was an electric under-floor cooling system that kept the carpet permanently cold. 'You're back,' said The Priestess. She snapped open a deckchair for me. I jumped in terror. 'It's just a chair,' she smirked but we both knew she'd done it on purpose. She sat, or swayed, in a child's swing with her legs through the leg-holes. She was tiny. 'You've come for a key?' 'Yes Priestess.' 'To unlock the heart of a beautiful maiden?' 'Yes Priestess.' I sat in the damp deckchair as she swung before me like a rancid pendulum. 'I've given you shitloads of keys. Aren't you bored yet?' 'This is the last one.' 'That's what you always say.' 'This time it's true.' 'You always say that too.' 'I never knew the meaning of love before.' 'And that.' 'I recently learnt a new word: transformative.' 'You have it tattooed on your neck.' 'Do I? I only learnt it two weeks ago!' I tried to look at my neck. 'It's like watching the same play over and over with a slightly older actress in the lead.' She threw me a rusty gold key. I caught it. I felt the blood rushing back. I felt my clitoris stabilise for a moment. 'Till next time, buster' she said. 'There won't be a next time!' we said together in perfect unison. 'Stop it I'm serious!' we shouted. 'Stop predicting my statements!' we shouted. I tried to say something original. 'What else can I trust except my feelings?' I said. I smiled triumphantly. She pressed play on her obscenely huge television. A cartoon squirrel was standing mournfully at the foot of a tree holding an acorn like a skull and soliloquizing: 'What else can I trust except my feelings?' The Priestess switched it off. 'Squirrel Hamlet,' she said. 'Did you create a whole cartoon show just to make that point?' I said. She threw a napkin at me with my question written on it. It fluttered like a boneless bird. She stopped her swing by punching the ground so hard she buried her fist. 'Anchor yourself,' she whispered.

THE TREE ROOM

Splayed out like walruses on the carpet,
we made Christmas decorations
as Cat Stevens sang
from the CD player kindly procured
by the counsellor. It was my first activity.
I'd come straight from detox
to 'The Tree Room' where Carli handed me
a Pritt-stick, two polystyrene balls
and a strip of googly-eye stickers.
Scott was an advertising mogul
for a famous soft drinks company.
He made an angel. *Oh baby baby it's a wild world.*
Carli had three estranged children,
was six weeks sober, bright-eyed and fit,
wore neon sportswear all day
and had long loud conversations
in the telephone-corner at night.
She made an ambitious red nosed reindeer
with pipe cleaner antlers. I remember
how warm it was in there.
I painted the polystyrene balls with glue
then wrapped them in cotton wool.
None of us spoke. I looked at them both,
foreheads furrowed,
glitter pens busy, big legs
tucked sideways beneath them.
My snowman was implausibly fluffy
and his eyes were too far apart
but Carli said 'cute.' I hung him
on a plastic branch. We sat and stared
at our handiwork, knees pulled up

to our chins. *A lot of nice things
turn bad out there.* I know what happened
after they left, the sad
violent details of their respective
returns to the world. I know the storm
I'm shaking with today. But then
we didn't know. *I'll always remember you
like a child, girl.* We were sheltered,
encased, forgiven, reduced
to a communal hum in a room
where our only purpose was to serve,
with childlike industry, the beauty
of a small fake tree.

LOVEBOROUGH

No one dies here or chews their food properly.
We break bread rolls in half and choke until we gulp.
We stay up all night talking animatedly to dial tones.
We hit small children whenever we gesticulate.

Occasionally someone faints and we hold a funeral
then applaud and cheer when they inevitably revive,
shouting 'It's a miracle!' We shout 'miracle' a lot:
when the coffee is drinkable, when the drizzle stops.

No one keeps receipts. Our tenement buildings
are modelled after comfortable Scandinavian prisons
so we get our groceries home delivered,
chill out most of the year, lightly repent.

Everyone has a running machine facing a blue wall.
The most beautiful woman in the world around here
is called Samantha and she loves me. She sent a letter
telling me so. I read it to my cactus and it flowered.

My yearning often paralyses me in my armchair
for entire days, the phone just rings and rings.
Samantha leaves long voicemails screaming 'Wake up!'
petrified I'm dead. She's adorable like that.

I'm an addict. I keep a pill on the roof of my mouth
but never swallow it. I will never swallow it.
No one dies here or grinds their pepper.
We pour peppercorns onto our pasta.

In our crumbling music halls, we sing about finality
and trail off before the last verse, laugh, pour a big wine.
We don't end relationships we let them overlap
indefinitely until we forget their names.

Christmas is a shit-show. Everything comes out.
We spend ages stuffing the lies back into ourselves.
Samantha wants to move to a different town.
She says our local traditions are 'enfeebling.'

Our quicksand foot spas. Our seated silent discos.
Our in-house pub crawls (just crawling around a pub.)
Our shame bracelets. She uses 'insidious' five times
in one sentence. She says she could love me forever

if I ran away with her to somewhere bright
with breathable fabrics, without the faces of ex-lovers
plastered on all the billboards plus their phone numbers;
a place where people are allowed to move on

get well, find a different answer to their lives.
'But I'm your answer,' I tell her, 'and you're mine.
Why would you want to find an answer that isn't me?'
She sighs and says 'Oh, Caroline' in that hurt twang

like I'm missing the point. I put on 'Suzanne'
by Leonard Cohen but she kicks the record player
shouting 'No! I will not 'touch your perfect body
with my mind'! I want a nourishing relationship!'

then storms out before I can feed her an orange.
I lie beneath the bubbles of my bath all day, breathing
through a curly straw. Samantha's not like the others.
She expects something from me. I wish I knew what.

THE INSURMOUNTABLES

Let's say
the married man with tears for eyes
made a talisman from a feather and a dead
butterfly
and burnt it in the corner of the garden

and far away, a woman
felt a burning, felt a cloud
pop in her ribs,
a sudden terrifying lightness in her hand;
jolted in her chair
like someone falling in a dream and
her husband said, what's wrong?
and she said

'nothing'

as the wings caught fire
and fire became flight and the dead
butterfly translated into smoke
and something was released back into the wild

and untrained air where love is born
before we take it home.

I AM NOT A FALCONER

I am standing in this field
Holding my glove in the air
Should I whistle?
I can't whistle
Will she get lost?
Take shelter in a charming tree?
It's starting to rain
Is that bad?
This is a woolly glove
Calm down
Falconers are patient
It's very windy
The sky is so big
She could be literally anywhere
Penzance
India
Why did I let her go?
I'm not a falconer!
Do I just keep standing here?
I'd go home and change
Into appropriate footwear
But what if I missed her?
I bet falcons are like Fedex
The second you nip to the loo...
What am I talking about?
A falconer doesn't get antsy
A falconer just knows
I lift my fist higher
If my arm gets tired I'll switch arms
Miss, miss!
Like I'm asking God a question

Please come back to me
Through the wind and rain
Come back
Even though you're free
I'm drenched
My glove is wrong
And you are not a falcon

FANCY DRESS

A hand in a glove costume
A wife in a traitor costume
A stranger in a hope costume
Your face in a listening costume
An expectant mother in an expectant mother costume
A phone call in a goodbye costume
A plea dressed as an anecdote dressed as a joke dressed
as doesn't matter dressed as never mind
Sex in a conversation costume
A hopelessness dressed as an action dressed as a mouth
dressed as a lie dressed as a confession dressed as bravery
A hopelessness in a bravery costume
A window in a sky poncho
A window holding up a large blue sign
A window getting changed behind a towel made of sky
A wooden table in a family costume
A nightmare in a reality costume
Our reality costumes are really, really good
The Sun rings the Moon's doorbell
Ding-dong. Party!
The Moon says to the Sun, 'What have you come as?'
'Darkness Man!' says the Sun
'Not again' says the Moon
'By day he's just average Sunny Ray but when night falls he becomes…'
'It's been 4.5 billion years mate, no one cares about Darkness Man'
'Watch this space'
'That is literally all I ever do'
A sadness in a wit costume
Sad mouths in long flowing robes of laughter
Sad eyes in attention masks
Sad voices in perky fascinators

An unwanted mental image in a physical tick costume
Masturbation in a respite suit
A fall in a getting up again costume
Photographs pretending to be real people smiling at you
The past tarted up like the present
Our present costumes are really, really good
Water in an ice costume (rent only)
Death in a meaning costume
Good lighting in a beauty costume
Infiltration in a giggle costume
A void dressed as a chock-a-block digital calendar complete
with actual appointments and perspiration hairspray
that induces real stress, in a passion hat
A marriage still wearing its passion hat
like a Christmas cracker paper crown on Boxing Day
Every single fucking day in a passion hat
You in a me costume
Me in a wisdom costume trying to staple the cloak to my skin
An evasion in an answer costume
Time dressed as a decent amount of itself
A closed door in an open door costume
Our open door costumes are really, really good
Have you ever seen a moment in the nude?
Of course not. Moments never remove their costumes
Not even in bed. If you were to see a naked moment
you would be appalled. Their bodies are clammy and vague
like half-finished sculptures. Never let them hold your hand
Their skin is silicone mould. Their palms will retain an imprint
of your fingerprints. Their hand will become yours
Moments are like spies or chameleons
Their voice is the breath that precedes a question that will never
reunite with its words. You wouldn't recognise
a moment outside of this fancy dress party
You'd probably mistake it for a patch of nothingness

'I'm always getting mistaken for a moment,' says the patch
of nothingness, 'It happens at least once a week. Strangers
on the street. Sometimes I'm so exhausted I just go along with it'
Likewise a moment is often mistakenly invited
to talk about nothingness on the radio
Air in a tension costume
Distance in a space between us costume
A little boy in a grown suit wearing old age makeup and liver spots
painted on his hands dressed as my granddad dressed as a final memory
dressed as a dying man wearing an it's-my-time costume
Our letting-go costume is biodegradable
and designed to disintegrate after a few wears
4am in a revelation costume
My face with the horizon drawn across it
A line in an ending costume, brand new, created for the occasion
with this nifty reversible lining, look: just turn inside out
and the ending transforms into the silence that follows

CHECKOUT

I think 'so, this is death' and wonder why
I can still see through my eyes. An angel
approaches with a feedback form asking
how I'd rate my life (very good, good,
average, bad, very bad) and I intend to tick
'average' followed by a rant then I recall
your face like a cartoon treasure chest
glowing with gold light, tick 'very good,'
and in the comment box below I write
'nice job.' The angel asks if I enjoyed
my stay and I say 'Oh yes, I'd definitely
come again' and he gives me a soft look
meaning 'that won't be possible but thanks
all the same,' clicks his pen and vanishes.

Do you remember the one about the bomber plane during World War II, riddled with bullets from enemy fire, and the plucky pilot who took five packs of Wrigley's peppermint gum from his pocket and told his crew to chew – 'Chew, Crew!' – so they chewed, ripping strip after strip from their foil sleeves to bung the bullet holes, plugging each perforation with a tooth-marked blob like a wax seal, wet and glistening, stamped with their personal crest. Six lads on the plane, or four, or five. Seven strips per pack – so that's thirty-five pieces of gum, it'd take at least three minutes, or maybe it'd just take a minute, their jaws would ache and they'd be ridiculously minty, smoke and fire out the window, planes spiralling down out of the sky, towards the ocean. I don't even know if that's how planes work, or if gumming punctures keeps you airborne. I guess you can't have all that wind shrieking through it. Well anyway it's not a true story. If it were true, you'd have heard of it, maybe I saw it in a cartoon. I like it because it's literally the only idea I'd have if asked to bung a bullet hole. We played our love like that for a while. Chewing then stoppering. A patch-up job cobbled in mid-air from whatever we had in our pockets at the time, fighting fire with blobs of miscellaneous optimism, aiming only for temporary insulation, to stopper the sky whistling through us, stay airborne, unofficial and miraculous, cork each new wound with a wad of sweetness freshly printed from the panic of our mouths.

We're trapped inside a movie. Apparently.
Last month 'the grand secret'
was disclosed to us via these giant faces
in the sky claiming to be 'producers' benevolently
dropping by to let us know we were
characters trapped inside their movie and
that every decision we made from now on
would be 'in the script' and therefore
we shouldn't blame ourselves too much or get
overly self-critical, some of us were villains,
some bit-parts, some heroes, but
everyone was 'necessary' for the story
and important in their own way, then the sky
went blank and everyone turned to each other
and made that sound crowds make
after receiving unexpected news: hubbub hubbub.
'We're in a movie! Of course!'
People kept shouting. 'It all makes sense now!'
'So that's why my shoes don't come off.'
'So that's why I'm always losing money
on the same horse.' 'So that's why I gel my hair
like a vampire, I *am* a vampire.'
'I knew I looked too young to be a grandma,'
said my grandma, 'What am I? Thirty-eight?'
They all seemed so reassured, so validated.
The next day, they resumed their roles
with gusto. The greengrocer started
throwing apples at children as a gesture
of goodwill and then winking.
My auntie began consciously 'bustling'
through doorways. Tramps cut the fingers

off their gloves, practised saying 'god bless us all'
then coughing in chorus. Nothing really changed
exactly, reality just got more pronounced
like someone underlined the word 'normal'
in our stage directions, you know? But...
I'm not buying it. 'Trapped inside a movie?'
What is this? Surrealism for beginners?
Yes I keep bursting into song
whenever the streetlights come on. Yes
I keep chasing the girl of my dreams
across New York. Yes we walk hand in hand
along the moonlit river as the disembodied
voice of Ella Fitzgerald drifts through
the glowing blossom trees but these are merely
facts and not the whole truth, I don't care
what 'the producers' in the sky say,
they're not in my heart, they don't know
the subtle earthquake of her eyes. I don't
care if there's a script with these lines
written in it, or some douchebags
throwing popcorn at a screen, I can't see
a screen, I can't see anything but her and
I need to tell her how I feel and my boat
leaves in the morning and she is
on the other side of Manhattan.

MID-AIR

There is a corner of the city where the air is
soft resin. Step in and it hardens
around you. We made
the mistake of kissing there. I mean, here.
Our mouths midway
across the same
inhalation like robbers mid-leap between
rooftops. If kisses were scored by composers
they'd place the breath on the upbeat. Oh
God. Music preceded by mid-air,
when the baton lifts, the orchestra tightens: 'And'
before the 'one two three.' And
the sunlight is meticulous. And the river
holds its tongue. And your silver
earring steels like an aerialist's hoop, caught
mid-spin. A note almost sung. Locked
in the amber of the and.
We just want to land or
be landed on.

NANCY AND THE TORPEDO

Nancy found an entire torpedo in the forest
just lying there like a beached whale,
coated in wet leaves
and decorated with glittering snail trails.
'It's a fucking torpedo,' she said.

'Is it... live?' I said.
I didn't know how torpedoes worked.
Were they like mines?

'It's inert,' she said, suddenly an expert,
'torpedoes don't explode on land,
everyone knows that.' She whistled like a plumber
surveying a damp patch, 'He's a beauty alright.
I reckon he weighs at least 600 pounds. 640, I'd say.'

'He?' I said, but Nancy was already straddling it,
spanking its rudder like the rump of a prize horse.
'What's a torpedo doing in a forest?'

Nancy rolled her eyes.
'You always ask the most obvious questions, don't you?
Can't you just enjoy the moment?'

She'd already unzipped her trousers
and was touching herself, grinding up
against the girth of the weapon
and groaning gently. 'Careful,' I said.

Her orgasm gathered to a scream.'
She pressed her sweating face
on the warhead and fell asleep on top of it.
The torpedo precisely matched the length of her body.

To my tired gaze, it seemed
as if they were *both* breathing,
Nancy and the torpedo, their chests
rising and falling together
like unsuspecting ocean waves.

I pictured them both in action,
underwater, Nancy's legs wrapped around
its speeding shaft, her red eyes fixed like sniper
dots on the target ahead, a string of bubbles
flying out behind her like a chiffon scarf.

Eventually she woke, refreshed and cheerful,
patted the torpedo goodbye, hoisted on her backpack
and we continued our journey
as if nothing had happened.

'Where are we going?' she'd ask, every ten minutes or so.
'We've just got to keep moving,' I'd reply, pointing
in some arbitrary direction and striding with purpose,
trying to channel the sexual energy
of a self-propelled missile, 'Keep on moving.'

The dread swished around my gums
like someone else's tongue. If I had owned a penis
it would've secretly shrivelled in my pants.
'We've passed this clearing before,' Nancy said.

'Different clearing,' I said. 'Those are our footprints
from four days ago,' she said. 'Different footprints,' I said.
Then we saw the torpedo. Nancy laughed.
'I suppose you're going to tell me that's a different torpedo?'

It was getting dark and cold. 'I love you. I just love you
so much,' I said, as Nancy remounted, hugging it
and whispering into its back, her mouth almost kissing
the metal. That's when I lost it.

'I'M SORRY I'M NOT A FUCKING TORPEDO!'

'I can't... blast through shit I'm
lost and I'm useless and I've got no fucking
idea where I am or what I'm doing. There. I said it.
Go ahead and dump me because I'm a piece of shit.'

There was a long silence.
Nancy straightened her spine like a dressage rider,
looked at me for an age then said,
'How many times do I have to prove it to you?'

'Prove what?' I said. She sighed,
'What could be more useless and impotent
than a dud torpedo in a forest?'

'I don't understand,' I said. She peeled a snail
from its propeller and threw it at me.
'I know exactly who you are,' she said,
slapping the steel, 'you and him
are headed in the same direction.'

'You mean, nowhere?'
She unzipped her trousers and reached down.
Fat tears appeared on her cheeks like rain. I didn't
understand why she was crying.

'You stupid idiot,' she said, her breath
quickening as she rubbed and grinded,
'Can't you see I'm doing this for you?
Can't you see I'm exploding for the both of us?'

DIVE BAR

Through a red door down a steep flight
of stairs into a windowless cellar
with sweating walls
an ingénue in a smoking jacket
sits atop a piano
as a host of swaying women
sing 'Your Secret's Safe with Me'
and one invites you
into the privacy of a kiss – all these
dark clandestine places – and you find
yourself imagining a very tiny
woman walking straight
into her mouth
through a red door down a steep flight
of throat into a windowless cell
with breathing walls
an ingénue in a smoke-jacket
sits astride a piano
as a host of swallowed women
sing 'Your Secret's in a Safe,'
the barmaid shakes a custom
cocktail she calls 'A Private Kiss'– all these
dark half-eaten faces – and you find
yourself imagining a tiny tiny
woman walking straight
into her mouth
through a red breath down a dark
thought into a swallowed sense
with shrinking walls
an innuendo in stomach acid
slops upon a piano

as a host of silent passions
mouth 'Your Secret is Yourself'
inside the belly of the world – all these
dark dissolving spaces – and you find
yourself imagining a windowless
woman breaking
walls down in herself, sprinting
up the shrinking
halls and up contracting
corridors and up the choking
fits of hard stares through dark
thoughts and dead
laws through the red door
as it swallows shut behind you
now you're spat out
on the pavement with the
sun just
coming out.

ROOKIE

You thought you could ride a bicycle
but, turns out, those weren't bikes
they were extremely bony horses. And that wasn't
a meal you cooked, that was a microwaved
hockey puck. And that wasn't a book that was
a taco stuffed with daisies. What if
you thought you could tie your laces?
But all this time you were just wrapping
a whole roll of sellotape round your shoe and
hoping for the best? And that piece of paper
you thought was your tax return?
A crayon drawing of a cat. And your best friend
is actually a scarecrow you stole from a field
and carted away in a wheelbarrow.
Your mobile phone is a strip of bark
with numbers scratched into it.
Thousands of people have had to replace
their doors, at much expense, after you
battered theirs to bits with a hammer
believing that was the correct way
to enter a room. You've been pouring pints
over your head. Playing card games with a pack
of stones. Everyone's been so confused
by you: opening a bottle of wine with a cutlass,
lying on the floor of buses, talking to
babies in a terrifyingly loud voice.
All the while nodding to yourself like
'Yeah, this is how it's done.'
Planting daffodils in a bucket of milk.

SPEECHLESS

It is such a relief for the words
they have been holding so much for so long
wrapped in furs like Russian soldiers
vowels crammed like backpacks, their lettered
backs are broken from it
syllables bent from all the shouldering
but tonight all the words left
the house in their thinnest summer
jackets, despite the December cold, they strutted
out with barely a stitch on
now they're shameless on the air, naked as a tune
sung by a sated ghost as she fades
from the drawing room into the bright
life where all business is complete.

Putting this Selected together was the loveliest, luckiest task. *And* it was also a bit like watching a breakdown in slow motion whilst strapped to a chair. Or sifting through a pile of confessional letters written in code and covered in old lipstick marks and scribbled phone numbers for long-since disconnected lines. It forced me to sit cross-legged in the attic of myself, meeting ghosts. And made me realise a few things for the first time.

One big thing I noticed is how often I subconsciously translated my relationships into surrealist vehicles in which I was miraculously heterosexual. It's funny how internalised shame can turn you into a surrealist because you're constantly trying to hide behind a wild, fantastical (yet ironically safer) scenario.

Even though people often associate poems with truth, I chose poetry because it let me hide and, once hidden, I could be brave, roll my heart in sequins and chuck it out, glittering, into the street. I could take the things I was ashamed of and translate them into dreams, turn drugs into fairy godmothers, breakdowns into tropical islands, depression into a wild horse with a clipboard; and feel protected...

I wasn't, of course, because the disguises became their own truths, and depression *is* a wild horse with a clipboard. Poetry is so tricksy like that: one minute you're running away from yourself and, suddenly, there you are.

Caroline Bird

ACKNOWLEDGEMENTS

Thank yous (from me and all the younger versions of myself in this book):

Michael Schmidt, my parents, my brother Robbie, my grand-parents, Tricia, Tony and Thomas, Barbara, Olivia and Juan, Simon Armitage, Phil Bowen, John Harrison, Peter and Ann Sansom, David Godwin, Philippa Sitters, Judith Wilson, Eleanor Crawforth, Andrew Latimer, Rodge Glass, Seanna Fallon, Rachel Long, Henry Stead, Leonora Wood, Mike McCarthy, Sarah Gillespie, Kathryn Maris, Hannah Silva, Elaine Feinstein, Monique Fare, Caroline Scott, Collette King, The Arvon Foundation, The Poetry Society, and everyone who has supported me since I was a child scribbling poems on a bean-bag wedged behind my bunk bed. My son Reece isn't old enough to read my books yet (thank goodness) but, for when he is: I love you! And thank you so, so much to my incredible wife-to-be, Eliza.